JEWISH
HOLIDAYS
AND
FESTIVALS

BY BEN M. EDIDIN
AUTHOR OF REBUILDING PALESTINE

ILLUSTRATED BY KYRA MARKHAM

HEBREW PUBLISHING COMPANY
NEW YORK

Republished by Omnigraphics ● Penobscot Building ● Detroit ● 1993

TO MY WIFE

Library of Congress Cataloging-in-Publication Data

Edidin, Ben M.
    Jewish holidays and festivals / Ben M. Edidin ; Kyra Markham,
illustrator.
       p. cm.
    Previously published: New York : Hebrew Pub. Co., c1940.
    Includes bibliographical references and index.
    ISBN 0-7808-0000-1 (lib. bdg. : alk. paper)
    1. Fasts and feasts—Judaism. I. Title.
BM690.E3   1993
296.4'3—dc20   93-2498
                                                CIP

∞

This book is printed on acid free paper meeting the ANSI Z39.48 Standard.
The infinity symbol that appears above indicates that the paper in this book
meets that standard.

Printed in the United States of America

Contents

INTRODUCTORY NOTE 7

CHAPTER   Page

   I *What Our Holidays Mean*   9

  II *The Sabbath* 17

 III *Rosh Hodesh* 35

 IV *The High Holy Days* 45

  V *Succot and Simhat Torah* 69

 VI *Hanukah, Festival of Lights* 87

VII *Hamishah Asar Bishevat* 105

VIII *Jolly Purim* 117

 IX *Pesach Then and Now* 131

  X *Lag Beomer* 155

 XI *Shavuot Festival* 165

XII *Tishah Beav and Other Fast Days* . . 179

XIII *New Anniversary Days* 189

XIV *The National American Festivals* . . 207

     BIBLIOGRAPHY 219

     INDEX AND GLOSSARY 221

Introductory Note

WRITING "Jewish Holidays and Festivals" has been truly a labor of love. Each chapter meant dipping into literary treasures, roaming over thousands of years of Jewish history, and taking imaginary flights to Jewish communities the world over. And as the book grew, the feeling of reverence for our holidays and the conviction of their significance to the American Jew became stronger within me. I hope that I have succeeded in conveying this reverence and conviction in a manner to inspire observance.

"Jewish Holidays and Festivals" is intended for home, school and club use. Parents will find it a handy source of information to read with their children and to answer questions. Teachers will find it a comprehensive textbook for classes on the junior and senior high school levels. To club leaders it should prove helpful as stimulating material for holiday programs and projects.

Grateful acknowledgment is hereby made to Dr. Leo L. Honor, Dr. Julius H. Greenstone, Mr. Ben Rosen, and Mr. Israel S. Chipkin, who read the original manuscript, for their helpful comments and suggestions.

A companion volume, "Jewish Customs and Institutions," treating the Jewish home, the synagogue, the personal religious events, and other aspects of Jewish observance, is scheduled for publication in the Summer of 1940.

B. M. E.

Chapter 1

WHAT OUR HOLIDAYS MEAN

THE JEWS have treasured and observed their holidays with extreme devotion ever since ancient times. We can hardly imagine Jewish life during the many centuries without Pesach, Yom Kippur, and the other holidays, without the weekly Sabbath, and without their beautiful customs and ceremonies. To every generation, these days brought beauty, cheer, and hope. To Jews in every land, they have served as constant reminders of great personalities and events in Jewish history, as symbols of lofty ideals and of religious beliefs, and as strong bonds uniting all Jews. It is doubtful whether the Jewish people could have survived the many centuries of wandering and persecution had they not observed their festivals and customs.

The holidays did not come into being all at once, of

9

course. Pesach, considered the oldest, originated as far back as three thousand years ago. Shavuot, Succot, Rosh Hashanah and Yom Kippur came later. As time went on and the Jewish people met with new experiences, Purim, Hanukah and Lag Beomer were added. The customs and ceremonies of each festival also developed gradually, in the course of many centuries. Even the meaning of certain holidays and customs changed as Jewish history marched(forward, for at all times the Jews have striven to make Jewish life joyous and purposeful.

OCCASIONS OF JOY

The Sabbath brings rest and joy and beauty to the Jewish home every week. The house seems different when mother kindles the lights. The Sabbath spirit, say our sages, enters the home at that very moment. Less often, but always welcome, come the holidays and festivals, each in its own season. On Rosh Hashanah and Yom Kippur all Jews seem more thoughtful and kindly. There is more tenderness among brothers, sisters, and friends. Hanukah brings lights, dreidels, parties. Purim unpacks hamantaschen, masks, and carnivals. Hamishah Asar means figs and dates, Palestine songs, and Horah dances. Pesach — but no need enumerating all. Each holiday is an important event in the life of a Jew. It is no wonder that being a Jew has meant so much to past generations and means so much today.

PAGES FROM THE PAST

Each holiday tells an important story from the long and eventful Jewish past. Pesach recalls the heroic exodus from

WHAT OUR HOLIDAYS MEAN

Egypt. Shavuot reminds us each year of the giving of the Ten Commandments, and brings back memories of farm-life in ancient Palestine. Succot recounts the journey to the Promised Land, and the agricultural festivals in Palestine. Hanukah tells of the Maccabees and their successful revolt against oppression; while Lag Beomer recalls an equally heroic revolt which unfortunately failed. Rosh Hashanah and Yom Kippur bring back vividly the ancient Temple ceremonies in Jerusalem. Purim recalls the Persian Haman and also his successors throughout the centuries, up to Hitler in our own day. While celebrating the holidays, the Jews of every generation felt themselves links in the long chain of Jewish history, carrying on the heritage and traditions of Israel.

SYMBOLS OF IDEALS

It may be that the festivals and ceremonies have lived on so long because they stand for certain ideals and aspirations cherished by the Jewish people.

Pesach stands for liberty and equality, and as such has it been observed all through the centuries. The Sabbath teaches freedom from another kind of slavery. A person who labors seven days a week, year in and year out, is a slave to his work. A day of rest, if properly spent, transforms one into a new person, refreshed, strengthened, ready to go on doing his best for family and community. Each one of the holidays and festivals represents some worthy ideal, as will be told throughout this book.

Even ceremonial objects have come to symbolize great ideals. The SHOFAR, blown on Rosh Hashanah and Yom Kippur, reminds Jews of the Messiah and of messianic times. When Messiah comes, Jews have believed, the words of Isaiah will come true:

"And the wolf shall dwell with the lamb,
And the leopard shall lie down with the kid,
And the calf and the young lion and the fatling together;
And a little child shall lead them.   Isaiah XL
For out of Zion shall go forth the law,
And the word of the Lord from Jerusalem.
And He shall judge between the nations,
And shall decide for many peoples;
And they shall beat their swords into plowshares,
And their spears into pruning-hooks;
Nation shall not lift up sword against nation,
Neither shall they learn war any more."

Isaiah II.

The MENORAH, kindled on the Sabbath and on holidays, is also more than an object for lighting candles. It is a symbol of light, telling how light and fire have helped mankind to advance from the life of primitive tribes to the kind we live today. It is also a symbol of light in the sense of wisdom and understanding — which are so important in the fight against cruelty, dishonesty, and other evils. The MENORAH represents purity as well. We act as we think and feel. If our thoughts and feelings are kindly and whole-hearted, then our acts are likely to be deeds of goodness and helpfulness.

FAITH AND HOPE

On holidays prayers are recited. What do these prayers contain? We need but open a prayerbook to discover at once the ideals which Jews have held dear all these centuries. Here are two selections:

> "Grant peace, welfare, blessing, grace, loving kindness, and mercy unto us."

> "Come, ye children, hearken unto me: I will teach you the fear of the Lord. What man is he that delighteth in life, and loveth many days that he may see good? Keep thy tongue from evil and thy lips from speaking guile. Depart from evil and do good; seek peace and pursue it."

Above all, the festivals and their ceremonies have helped to maintain the religious ideal of belief in God, in one God. This is best expressed in that three thousand years old cry: "Hear O Israel, the Lord is our God, the Lord is One." How many Jews throughout the centuries have died for their faith with these words on their lips!

UNITING BONDS

What is it that makes of scattered Israel one people? There are many bonds of unity — religion, history, the Bible and other literature, the Hebrew language. The holidays, too, are an important bond. Every Friday evening of the year, in millions of Jewish homes, candles are lit and the KIDDUSH recited. On millions of Jewish doorposts the little MEZUZAH bids you welcome. People who observe similar customs, at the same time, cannot help but feel united with one another. Every Jew who sits at the SEDER on Pesach night feels himself a brother of the millions of other Jews who chant the Haggadah at that hour. There is always a strong-

JEWISH HOLIDAYS AND FESTIVALS

er spirit of kinship among Jews because they celebrate the same festivals and observe similar customs.

FORCES FOR JEWISH SURVIVAL

If not for the holidays and customs, perhaps there would be no Jewish people today. Suppose that Jews had forgotten their history. In several generations very few Jews would have remained in the world. The customs and ceremonies, as told before, have served as constant lessons in Jewish history. What if the scattered Jews of the world had not been united in religious observance? The Jews of Morocco would soon have assimilated and become like Arabs. The Jews who first settled in Poland would have met a similar fate among the Poles. Those in Spain and Portugal would not have been burned at the stake by the Inquisition had they been willing to abandon the Sabbath and the holidays.

When do Jews usually meet for social purposes? When do families and friends customarily visit one another? They meet most often on holidays, on Friday evenings, and at special ceremonies such as a BAR MITZVAH. The proper observance of the festivals requires building of synagogues and organization of congregations, essential institutions of the Jewish community. Thus, by fostering fellowship and community life, the holidays have played an important role in the survival of the Jewish people.

The holidays and ceremonies meant so much to our forefathers throughout the ages that they were willing to suffer rather than cease observing them. Every father felt himself a king and every mother a queen on Sabbath evening. PESACH brought the beautiful SEDER. PURIM meant carnivals, masquerades, and parties. ROSH HASHANAH and YOM KIPPUR meant days of prayer and inspiration. Being a Jew was considered a God-given privilege, and the holidays and ceremonies were accounted His gifts. To give them up was unthinkable.

The Jews of today continue to observe the holidays and customs. To many Jews, however, they do not seem to mean so much as in past generations. Others try to observe them as beautifully as ever. In Palestine, where a new Jewish life is developing, old customs are being revived and new ones added. What is the history of each holiday and festival? Why have they meant so much to Jews through-

out the ages ? How were they celebrated in ancient Palestine, and in diaspora lands throughout the ages ? How are
they observed by Jews in various lands today ? What are
American Jews doing to strengthen the observance of the
Sabbath and the holidays? The devotion of Jews to the festivals and customs depends largely on how well they understand the answers to questions such as these.

Chapter 2

THE SABBATH

How happy Jews have been with the Sabbath and how thankful for it during countless centuries! No toil was too mean and no hardship too great during the entire week if only the last day was a real Sabbath—a day of rest, a day of joy, a day of freedom. Persecution became more bearable and exile less painful because of the blessed SHABBAT. The number of Jews who have died rather than break the Sabbath during the past three thousand years mounts into the hundreds of thousands.

Of our many holidays and observances, the Sabbath is the only one prescribed in the Ten Commandments, for it is one of the very first customs observed by our ancestors. It was celebrated as far back as Exodus days. You remember that when the Israelites were in the desert, journeying to the Promised Land, a double portion of manna was gathered on Friday. Even more important, the Fourth Commandment is the first labor law known to mankind. Two explanations are given in the Commandments for keeping the Sabbath. One is the religious reason—that God rested on the seventh day after having created the world in six days. The other is historical—because the Israelites were freed from slavery in Egypt.

The Jews were the first people in the world to celebrate the Sabbath as a day of rest and joy. The ancient Babylonians also observed the seventh day, but they considered it one of evil spirits and bad luck, because it seemed to them that the moon stands still every seventh day as it changes from one phase to another. This being an evil day, they stayed indoors and refrained from finishing any piece of work or beginning any new undertaking. How different were the ideas of our ancestors regarding the Sabbath—not a period of evil but a holy day of rest to be celebrated with gladness and ceremony, when man may feel free from the labors and worries of every day life. Centuries later, this great idea of the Sabbath was adopted by the Christians, and still later by the Moslems. The Sabbath is one of Israel's great contributions to the world.

The Sabbath in Ancient Times

Just how the Sabbath was observed at home in ancient times we do not know surely. It was evidently kept, in the main, by abstaining from heavy labor. Only the most necessary house and farm chores were done. We gather from the Bible that it was the favorite day for consulting the prophets and other wise men.

More is known of the Sabbath ceremonies in the Temple at Jerusalem. Fresh oil was poured into the large seven-branched MENORAH, and the lights were kindled anew, while twelve freshly baked HALLOT or shew-bread, one for each tribe, were placed on the altar. Then fragrant incense was burned. The eastern gate of the Temple was opened early in the morning and kept open all day so that people could come in freely to pray and watch the ceremonies. These rites consisted of animal and grain sacrifices, accompanied by hymns played and sung by the Levites. At the king's palace, the royal guard was changed on the seventh day.

As time went on the Sabbath became more and more important. The prophets and priests taught the people its meaning and observance. The rise of synagogues helped greatly to strengthen Sabbath loyalties. Now the people had a place where they could meet to pray, chant psalms, read portions of the Bible, and listen to the SOPHERIM or Scribes, as the teachers of the period were known. By the time of the Maccabees, the day had become so sacred that Jews chose to be burned alive rather than defend themselves on the Sabbath. The people had to be convinced that this was wrong, and that when life is in danger the Sabbath may be broken.

Sabbath in the Talmud

When the Talmud was completed, about 500 C.E., most of the customs and ceremonies known today were already observed and the meaning of the Sabbath was fully understood. In fact, two whole books of the Talmud are devoted to the Sabbath, in addition to the hundreds of stories, explanations, and sayings contained in other tractates and in the Midrashim.

In the eyes of those generations the Sabbath overshadowed all the other holy days, even Yom Kippur. It was considered God's own gift to the Jewish people, a precious jewel, as beautiful as a queen, as lovely as a bride. One sage said, "Great is the Sabbath, for it outweighs all the other MITZVOT." Another said, "He who rests on the Sabbath forgets all his troubles." "The Sabbath improves a person's character," proclaimed a third.

The Talmud asks, "How is SHABBAT to be observed?" And it answers, "With prayer and study, with good food and drink, with clean and becoming clothes, with rest and joy." Eating three good meals is actually prescribed in the Talmud as a religious duty. In the synagogues, there were sermons and discussions. Fragrant myrtle branches were used to decorate the home. If any fast day, excepting YOM KIPPUR, falls on the seventh day of the week, it must be postponed to the following day. Mourning is prohibited too, even for a close relative. Sabbath rest, declare the sages of the Talmud, distinguishes the Jews from other peoples, and is therefore necessary for the very survival of the Jewish people.

Sabbath in the Middle Ages

Centuries passed. The Jews scattered far and wide over the face of the earth. But at all times and in all lands, they clung firmly to the Sabbath. New ceremonies, customs, and prayers were added to the old. It became the day for many family events of a happy nature. The bridegroom was called up to the Torah on the Sabbath after the wedding. A newly born girl-child was named in the synagogue; the BAR

MITZVAH ceremony was held on the Sabbath. A person saved from danger offered a special prayer of thanksgiving on that day. EREV SHABBAT was the time for giving charity.

It was observed with equal devotion in times of peace and in lands of freedom as in periods of darkness and countries of persecution. Thus in Spain, during the Golden Age, the Sabbath was celebrated with no less fervor than in Christian lands during the terrible days of the Crusades. At all times and in all places, it was a day of joy, of rest, and of study. Even instrumental music was allowed, if played by non-Jews. Games, too, were permitted, chess being especially popular; and so was dancing. It was far from the "blue Saturday" which so many think the Sabbath to have been in former generations. We must remember that in those days the vast majority of people in every country were slaves who toiled endlessly. One does not wonder that the Jews were so happy that their religion bade them rest one day a week.

A TRADITIONAL SABBATH

As we come nearer to our own times, we find that the Sabbath is observed with greater care and devotion than ever before. Let us pay an imaginary visit to a Jewish home where the Sabbath is celebrated in the traditional manner. There are hundreds of thousands of such homes in the world today. Let us see how they prepare for SHABBAT, how Friday is spent, how Saturday is enjoyed, and how Queen Sabbath is bidden farewell.

Preparing for Sabbath

First on the list of preparations for Sabbath is shopping. The very best of everything is made ready. The poor skimp and pinch all week in order to enjoy the three Sabbath meals. Fish is always among the purchases, which already in ancient times was a favorite Sabbath dish. You may have read the talmudic tale of a poor Jew who outbid a wealthy Roman for the last fish in the market, and how the Jew was rewarded by finding a precious jewel inside the fish.

House-cleaning is next. By Friday morning the house is spic and span. The candlesticks, polished brightly, are in view, as if to announce that SHABBAT will soon be here. The best clothes are put in order, ready for wear. In the oven, the HALLOT or Sabbath loaves are baking. These represent a continuation of the ancient Temple custom, when the twelve loaves of shewbread on the altar were renewed in honor of the Sabbath. Two HALLOT are used to remind us of the double portion of manna gathered on Fridays.

By Friday noon, business and traffic are practically at a standstill in this Jewish community. Schools, too, close at noon. Every one hurries to get ready, for it is a MITZVAH to begin the Sabbath early and to enjoy more of it. An hour or two before sundown, a sacred hush prevails, interrupted only for a few moments by the blowing of a trumpet reminding one and all not to tarry, for the Sabbath is nigh. Quietly and cheerfully Jews are putting the finishing touches to their preparations. A final important act is dropping some coins into the charity box, usually by the youngest of the family.

Welcoming the Sabbath at Home

Mother is the first to bid official welcome to the Sabbath. As the sun disappears behind the horizon, she lights the candles and recites the appropriate blessing, adding a personal prayer for her family. This custom, too, dates back to Temple days, when the seven-branched MENORAH was filled with fresh oil and relit in honor of the day. Mother usually lights one candle for each member of the family; in some homes the seven-branched MENORAH is illumined. Father and children stand by quietly and answer Amen. As she finishes, every one feels that the Sabbath has arrived. The house has changed. Something sacred has entered it, to stay for a full twenty-four hours.

In the Synagogue

The father and sons go to synagogue, there to welcome the Sabbath with public prayer. But first father places his hands gently on the heads of the children and blesses them. One of the prayers of welcome chanted at the synagogue service is "Lechah Dodi," composed by a Jew of Safed, Palestine, only three hundred years ago. "Come, my friend, to meet the bride, to welcome the Sabbath," the congregation chants in unison. At the conclusion of the service, the KIDDUSH is recited by the HAZAN, for the sake of those who have no families and cannot say it at home. The KIDDUSH reminds the people of the two reasons for observing the Sabbath—the creation of the world and liberation from slavery in Egypt.

Sabbath greetings are exchanged, and every one walks home serenely and cheerfully. SHABBAT SHALOM or GUT SHABBOS is the greeting; SHABBAT SHALOM UVERACHAH or GUT SHABBOS GUT YOHR is the reply. Many are accompanied by strangers or poor people, for it is the custom to have a guest at the table, so that all may enjoy the Sabbath meals properly. A legend tells that two angels accompany them home, an angel of goodness and an angel of evil. If there is peace and harmony in the family, the good angel says, "So

23

may it be next SHABBAT." If not, the angel of evil has his inning, while the good one hangs his head in shame.

The Evening Meal

SHABBAT SHALOM or GUT SHABBOS, says father as he enters the house, upon his return from the synagogue. The table is set with the family's best china and silverware. The two HALLOT are at the head of the table, covered with an embroidered napkin. The candlesticks stand in the center, and near them the KIDDUSH cup. As mother busies herself putting the last touches to the table, father recites the famous chapter in Proverbs, "A Woman of Worth," a poem of praise to her. Then he and the boys chant SHALOM ALEICHEM, a hymn which begins with the words, "Peace be unto you, angels of peace."

Now the family is seated at the table. The meal begins with the KIDDUSH. Then father cuts one HALLAH, giving every one a slice. Before it is eaten, the blessing HAMOTZI is pronounced. At last the meal is served—fish, soup, chicken, tzimes, stewed fruit, and other Sabbath favorites.

Zemirot

Between one course and another, ZEMIROT are sung—songs of thanksgiving for the blessed Sabbath. There are many ZEMIROT, and singing at meal time has become one of the distinctive Sabbath customs. They add much to the spirit and joy of the day. There are special songs for Friday evening, for Saturday noon, and for the SEUDAH SHELISHIT or third meal. The meal is concluded with BIRKAT HAMAZON, or grace.

The rest of the evening is spent quietly. Father reads over the portion or SIDRAH of the week — twice in the original

Hebrew and once in the Aramaic translation. Mother, too, after clearing the table and washing the dishes, looks into the Pentateuch or the prayerbook. The children read, go out for a short walk, or play quiet games. Sometimes relatives and neighbors drop in and are welcomed with refreshments.

Sabbath Day

In the morning the town lies quiet and peaceful, as men, women, and children walk leisurely to the synagogue. The service is chanted in a melody reserved for the Sabbath. Between the SHAHARIT and MUSAF prayers, the Torah Scroll is taken out and read. At least seven men are called up. Two more receive the honor of lifting and dressing the Scroll, while another is privileged to chant the prophetic reading, or HAFTORAH. Quite often a Bar Mitzvah boy, a bridegroom, or some person who has a special reason for being happy, chants the HAFTORAH. Sometimes a visiting HAZAN entertains the congregation. Occasionally, a MAGGID or preacher delivers a sermon. On all such Sabbaths, the service is especially enjoyable.

The noon meal also begins with a short KIDDUSH. The food served is again of the best, and is enjoyed by every one, though cooked the day before. ZEMIROT are sung, in greater number than on the preceding night.

In the afternoon, the older folks take a nap, while the children and young folks go out to play. The school boys, however, must be back for their weekly test as soon as father wakes up. Often it is grandfather who gives the examination. In some communities, the children come to school for an hour or so to read the Ethics of the Fathers and be entertained with stories. The favorite pastime of the young folks is promenading. The sidewalks of the main avenue are crowded with gay strollers all afternoon. Many families are visiting one another. Later in the day, father attends synagogue to listen to a speaker or to take part in one of the several study groups. After that, he joins in the MINHAH or afternoon service.

Seudah Shelishit

In a corner of the room, a long table is being set for the third Sabbath meal or SEUDAH SHELISHIT. As the sun begins to set, the men sit down for the "feast." Wise sayings are expounded, stories and anecdotes related. Every one partakes of the food and drink. But what makes this occasion most enjoyable are the songs, usually songs without words, expressing joy and sorrow, hope and longing. This SEUDAH concludes with the HAVDALAH ceremony and with general wishes for a happy week.

Mother and the children bid farewell to the Sabbath at home. The mother chants "God of Abraham" as she goes about arranging things for the evening ahead. In this song she offers thanks for the holy Sabbath and prays for health and happiness for her family and for all Israel.

Havdalah Ceremony

Soon father returns. The family gathers around him for the HAVDALAH ceremony. One child holds the twisted candle, while another holds the BESAMIM or spice box. Father raises the goblet of wine, or a glass of milk, as he chants the prayers thanking God for the Sabbath and for the days of work, and asking for light and joy and gladness and honor. He inhales the fragrance of the spices and recites a blessing for the good things in life. He brings his hands close to the

26

light, bending his fingers to make a shadow, so as to distinguish between light and darkness, and he offers thanks to God for creating light. With the greeting, GUT WOCH, Happy Week, he concludes the ceremony. But the Sabbath spirit lingers on as the family sings several melodies, the favorite song being about Elijah and the Messiah.

Melaveh Malkah

HASIDIM bid farewell to the Sabbath again later in the evening, with a ceremony called MELAVEH MALKAH or Farewell to the Queen, held usually at the rabbi's home. They eat and drink, tell stories from Jewish lore, sing songs of joy and devotion, and dance hasidic dances. The rabbi speaks to them on subjects from the Torah and the Talmud, and on the teachings of great hasidic leaders.

Special Sabbaths

While every Sabbath is festive and inspiring, several are especially important. On SHABBAT HAGADOL, before PESACH, the approach of the beautiful festival is already sensed. On SHABBAT HAZON, before TISHAH BEAV, a mood of sadness prevails; while on the following Sabbath, in contrast, the prophecy of hope which begins "Comfort ye, comfort ye, my people" is chanted. This Sabbath is known as SHABBAT NAHAMU or Sabbath of Comforting. The Sabbath before Hamishah Asar Bishevat is called SHABBAT SHIRAH, the Sabbath of Song, for the famous poem of victory over Egypt is read on that day. Still another special Sabbath is the one between Rosh Hashanah and Yom Kippur, known as SHABBAT SHUVAH, Sabbath of Repentance. One Sabbath each month, when the new month is announced, is called SHABBAT MEVARCHIM. In addition to these, many Sabbaths are especially festive because of Bar Mitzvahs, births, and other personal ceremonies celebrated in the synagogue.

SABBATH IN MANY LANDS

The Sabbath described in the preceding pages is observed by orthodox Jews in Europe, in Palestine, and in America. What of the Oriental Jews living in Asia, Africa, and certain Mediterranean countries in Europe? And how is SHABBAT observed in Palestine? Oriental Jews are on the whole very pious; and they observe the Sabbath with extreme devotion. Some of their customs seem to us rather severe, while others appear quaint.

Donning clean fresh clothes in honor of the Sabbath is observed by Orientals even more than by Europeans. Bagdad Jews would not think of welcoming the Sabbath in week-day clothes. Kurdistan Jewish men wear short trousers and go barefoot all week. But on the Sabbath they put on clean long robes and are careful not to walk barefoot. Yemenite Jews dress in clean white linens.

The strictest observers of the Sabbath are the Karaites,* the Samaritans, and the Falashas* of Abyssinia. On Friday nights they sit in the dark. Is it not written in the Bible, they explain, "Ye shalt not kindle any light in your dwellings"? For the same reason they eat only cold foods on Saturday. They also interpret the biblical commandment, "Thou shalt not go out of the threshold of your home," very strictly and stay indoors all day, allowing themselves only a short walk to and from synagogue. The Falashas consider SHABBAT

---

* The Samaritans are not considered Jews. They, as well as the Karaites and Falashas, have not accepted the teachings of the Talmud. As a result, the Sabbath has not been for them a day of joy as for the rest of Jewry.

28

more important than Yom Kippur, and when Yom Kippur happens to fall on Saturday, they eat lightly.

In contrast, among the native Jews of India, known as Bene Israel, many work on the seventh day. But first they come to synagogue and then have their Sabbath meal at home. In the synagogue, only those who keep the Sabbath strictly and abstain from work are called up to the Torah.

In Yemen, the reading of the Torah takes two hours and even more. Instead of one person reading the SIDRAH or portion of the week every one present reads all of it aloud to the others. After each chapter, a young boy translates and explains it in Arabic. Small wonder that most of the Yemenite Jews know the Pentateuch by heart. The afternoon is spent in the synagogue, with reading and joint study of the Bible and other sacred books.

We find quaint customs also among the Marranos of Portugal. They eat only fish, vegetables, and fruit on SHABBAT, since they usually are unable to obtain KOSHER meat, and on the Sabbath they want to be especially careful. The morning service, recited three times instead of only once, takes place in a home where family and friends gather to pray. Before they light the candles on Friday, several prayers are said imploring God to spare them undue suffering.

An interesting custom among the Jews of Egypt is consolation of mourners. After the service, the rabbi and leaders of the congregation come to the mourner's seat and chant psalms of consolation to him. Then they proceed to the home of the bereaved to console the rest of the family in like manner.

The blessing of children on Friday is also a common custom among Oriental Jews. In Saloniki, Greece, every member of the family comes up to the master of the house after the KIDDUSH and kisses his hand.

Shabbat in Palestine

The one most important Sabbath custom, rest from work, is observed by all Jews in Palestine. Offices, factories, stores, schools, theatres—everything is closed. Only a few restaurants keep open during certain hours to serve meals to those who have no families, and a drug store or two for emergency prescriptions. On the farms, of course, the livestock is fed, the cows are milked, and other such chores are performed. Public traffic stops about an hour before sunset on Friday, and is not resumed until an hour after sunset the following day. The absence of traffic helps to create a spirit of quiet and peacefulness.

A new Palestinian custom is flowers for the Sabbath. All Friday afternoon men, women, and children carry bouquets wherewith to decorate their homes. Florists are permitted to keep open later so that no one may be deprived of this new MITZVAH.

By dusk, candle light glitters in every home. A little later the tunes of ZEMIROT and new Hebrew songs come streaming through open windows, and from the balconies where many eat in warm weather. After the dinner hour, the streets begin to fill with strollers. The young people sing and play mouth organs as they walk. Some are on their way to parties, lectures, or "sings."

On Saturday morning the synagogues are crowded with worshippers. In the old city of Jerusalem, groups continue streaming all morning through the narrow, winding streets towards the Wailing Wall, for pious Jews consider it a special privilege to worship at the sacred wall, and they come to complete the MUSAF service there. Halutzim and tourists also come then to pay their respects to this sacred site.

SHABBAT afternoon is the time for visiting relatives and friends, for meetings and lectures, for games and sings, for promenading, or for quiet reading at home. Youth organizations, like the Scouts, spend the afternoon in their club houses and on the play fields. Sport fans, young and old, watch soccer games, even though the very pious frown upon such Sabbath recreation. In Tel Aviv and Haifa the beaches are crowded with bathers on summer Sabbaths.

Oneg Shabbat

About two hours before sunset, hundreds of people gather in public halls for a new Sabbath custom, originated some fifteen years ago by the great Hebrew poet Bialik. It is called ONEG SHABBAT, Sabbath Joy, and combines the old customs of group study, SEUDAH SHELISHIT, and HAVDALAH.

31

Jewish Holidays and Festivals

The program begins with a lecture and discussion. Then, as the sun dips to the horizon, the audience sings ZEMIROT, hasidic tunes, and new Hebrew melodies. Last comes the HAVDALAH ceremony. This ONEG SHABBAT custom has spread to many other countries, including the United States.

Sabbath in America

In America the Sabbath is not observed by all Jews alike. In thousands of homes it is kept in the traditional manner, while in many others only part of the customs are observed. But there are very few Jewish homes indeed where the Sabbath spirit is not felt to some extent on Friday evenings and also on Saturdays.

In countless thousands of American Jewish homes, the Sabbath is a true family festival, bringing members of the family closer together. All week every one is busy. On Friday night, young and old relax. The candle light, the good food, the songs and prayers, all create a warm, peaceful atmosphere. Every one seems more kindly and more considerate. This is what our sages meant when they said that on SHABBAT one has a NESHAMAH YETERAH, an over-soul.

After the festive meal, the family spends the evening quietly at home. Some go to the synagogue for the late services. The late Friday evening service is a new Sabbath custom which has arisen in America during recent years.

In the morning, those able to abstain from work go to synagogue to pray, listen to the rabbi's sermon, and meet friends. The noon meal is eaten leisurely, with ZEMIROT between courses. The afternoon is spent in reading, playing quiet games, visiting friends, attending a museum, going for a walk, or just lounging at home. There are many enjoyable

32

and interesting things which do not require the use of money or traveling or boisterous play. After sunset, the HAVDALAH ceremony is performed in the home. Jewish institutions and organizations occasionally hold a MELAVEH MALKAH.

To American Jews, too, the Sabbath serves as a reminder and symbol of the finer things in life. All week we are preoccupied with school, with house duties, with business, with making a living. SHABBAT is the time to think of ideals and of better ways of living, for the Sabbath stands for personal happiness and for the achievement of a better social order. The great Jewish thinker, Ahad Haam, has said, "More than the Jews have kept the Sabbath, the Sabbath has kept the Jewish people."

Questions of Thinking Jews

Many American Jews who appreciate the importance and beauty of the Sabbath would like to enjoy it as their parents and grandparents did, but find themselves unable to keep all the customs and ceremonies of the traditional Sabbath. This makes them unhappy, and anxious to correct the situation. Every time they examine the old customs thoughtfully, they find that they are as beautiful and worthwhile today as in the past. Why cannot a modern Jewish family light the Sabbath candles and have a joyous meal with KIDDUSH and ZEMIROT on Friday evenings? Why cannot the rest of the evening be spent quietly at home, in reading Jewish books and magazines, discussing Jewish topics, singing Jewish songs, and playing games? Or at the synagogue for late Friday services?

And what of Saturday? Many do not work on this day and can go to synagogue. Women and children certainly are free to attend. Many work only until noon and can spend the rest of the day in the true Sabbath spirit. Why should not every family bid farewell to the Sabbath with HAV-DALAH? Clubs and family circles can gather in the afternoon for an ONEG SHABBAT. Occasionally a MELAVEH MALKAH may be held in the evening.

Many of these thinking Jews look to Palestine to learn how the Sabbath can be observed in modern times. Some of the customs and ceremonies can be changed and adapted. Surely the Jews of America will find a way of preserving the precious gift which from the very beginning has been so important in the life of the Jewish people.

Chapter 3

ROSH HODESH

You may remember David's remark to Jonathan when the two were troubled about Saul's anger against David: "Behold, tomorrow is the new moon, when I should sit with the king to eat." Saul evidently observed the first of each month, or ROSH HODESH, with a family feast, to which a lesser member of the court might also be invited. Some scholars believe that at one time ROSH HODESH was even more important than the Sabbath as a day of rest and festivity.

When the laws of the Bible were written down, the observance of ROSH HODESH was definitely prescribed: "And in your new moons ye shall blow with the trumpets over the sacrifices of your peace-offerings." In another chapter we find a description of the ceremony and of the sacrifices in the Temple on that day. We can obtain an idea of how joyous and important an occasion ROSH HODESH was in ancient times from one of the psalms:

> Sing aloud unto God our strength;
> Shout unto the God of Jacob.
> Take up the melody, and sound the timbrel,
> The sweet harp with the psaltery.
>
> Blow the horn at the new moon,
> At the full moon for our feast day.
> For it is a statute for Israel,
> An ordinance of the God of Jacob.
>
> (Psalms LXXXI, 2-5)

Announcing the New Month

The moon occupied an important place in the life of our ancestors in Palestine. It was their guide to the calendar. They counted months and days by the moon and often made appointments for when the moon would be in a certain shape and position. The appearance of the tiniest crescent meant the beginning of another month, and it was announced with blowing of the SHOFAR and with fire signals.

The power to announce the new month was vested in persons of authority. At the time of the First Temple, most likely the high priest or the king had this power. In the days

36

of the Second Temple, we know definitely, the Sanhedrin announced the new moon and set the dates of the holidays.

How was ROSH HODESH determined and proclaimed by the Sanhedrin? On the last day of the month, persons in Jerusalem would watch for the appearance of the new moon. The head of the Sanhedrin, with several of the elders, were assembled in the Temple courtyard to wait for the news. Those first to notice the slightest crescent rushed to the Temple with this information. The Patriarch questioned the witnesses as to the position, size, and shape of the crescent. When he was convinced that the evidence was correct, the SHOFAR would be blown and the beginning of the month announced.

That night torches and bonfires would be lit on the highest peaks near the city. These were signals to nearby towns and villages that the new month had been officially declared. The people in these places would in turn light bonfires and torches as signals to more distant settlements. These, in like manner, would notify still farther parts of the country. All night long, the fire signals carried the news, until the whole country was informed. The following day was celebrated as ROSH HODESH. Even the Jews of Babylonia were informed of the new moon by a relay of torches and bonfires. To more distant countries, like Egypt, Rome, and Persia, messengers were sent to apprise them of the exact dates of ROSH HODESH and of the holidays.

Two Days of Holiday

Traveling in those days was difficult and even dangerous, so that the messengers did not always arrive on time. The

* The Sanhedrin was both the supreme court and the legislative body of the Jewish nation at that time.

Jews in foreign countries often found themselves at a loss as to the exact days of the holidays during that month. In such instances they would observe two days, for one of the two was certain to be correct. Thus arose the custom of celebrating two days of ROSH HASHANAH, PESACH, SHAVUOT, and SUCCOT. When the Jewish calendar was later written down, this custom was retained for the Jews living outside of Palestine, and has become part of Jewish tradition, to this day. In Palestine, only one day is observed. Reform Jews, too, keep only one day.

Occasion of Thanksgiving

One of Palestine's neighbors was Babylonia, now called Iraq. There, too, the waxing and waning of the moon meant a great deal to the people. But these changes were feared rather than awaited with joy. The days between one moon and the next were considered a period of bad omen. On the night of full moon, the people kept indoors, believing that evil spirits then roved the earth.

To the Jews, in contrast, the reappearance of the moon meant joy and hope. They did not know as much about the universe and astronomy as we today, and they were not certain whether the moon, after disappearing from view, would come back again. When it did reappear, they were grateful and happy. Everything that is of benefit to human beings, the Jews recognized by thanksgiving and celebration. When the first fruits appeared on the trees, our ancestors marked them and brought them to the Temple on SHAVUOT as an offering.

In ancient times, then, ROSH HODESH was an occasion of thanksgiving, observed as a day of rest from work, and celebrated with ceremonies in the Temple at Jerusalem, and with family feasts throughout the country.

Changes in Observance of Rosh Hodesh

After the Temple was burned down by the Romans and sacrifices could no longer be offered, the manner of observing ROSH HODESH naturally changed. Instead of sacrifices, special prayers were recited in the synagogues and at home, including the hymns chanted in the Temple. However, the Sabbath was now far more important than ROSH HODESH in the life of the people.

Some three centuries after the destruction of the Temple, the Jewish calendar was set down in writing by Hillel the Second. Now it was no longer necessary to announce the new moon with blowing of the SHOFAR and with fire-signals. Jews no longer had to wait anxiously for word from Jerusalem as to when the months began and as to the dates of the festivals. They needed merely to consult the calendar.

Nevertheless, ROSH HODESH has remained an important occasion to this day, since the chief reason for the festival remained—appreciation for the return of the good things in life. Not only did the festival itself continue to be celebrated but the Sabbath before ROSH HODESH became one of the special Sabbaths of the year. In time, new prayers and ceremonies were added. Let us describe briefly how ROSH HODESH was observed by all Jews a hundred years ago, and how it is still observed in thousands of Jewish communities throughout the world.

The Sabbath Before

In ancient times the new moon was announced by the Sanhedrin in the Temple. Today the ceremony is performed in the synagogue on the Sabbath before ROSH HODESH, immediately after the reading of the Torah. First the congregation is informed of the MOLAD, or the exact time when the new moon is to appear. Then the HAZAN chants: "ROSH HODESH (naming the month) will be on (naming the day or days). May it come to us and to all Israel for good." The congregation repeats the sentence.

This announcement is preceded and followed by appropriate prayers, asking for peace, health, plenty, goodness, and understanding, and for the speedy rebuilding of Palestine. Following is the concluding prayer:

> "May the Holy One, blessed be He, renew the month for us and all His people, the house of Israel, for life and peace, for gladness and joy, for salvation and consolation, and let us say Amen."

On Rosh Hodesh Day

On ROSH HODESH proper we are again reminded of the ceremonies in the ancient Temple. Instead of sacrifices, however, prayers are recited, among them the famous Hallel prayer, which consists of selections from the Book of Psalms, expressing praise of God, thanksgiving, and hope. Before the MUSAF service, a portion of the Bible is read in the synagogue, as on the Sabbath.

In the home, ROSH HODESH is recognizable in two ways. Women usually abstain from sewing and other work which can be postponed. Men, too, follow this practice. The other variant is the meal, which is more festive than on regular week days.

ROSH HODESH is observed on one or two days. When the previous month has twenty-nine days, one day of ROSH

HODESH is celebrated; when the preceding month has thirty days, ROSH HODESH consists of two days. In the latter case, the first day of the New Moon is the thirtieth day of the previous month. Very pious Jews fast on the day before ROSH HODESH and pray for forgiveness. In fact, they consider it a minor YOM KIPPUR.

New Moon Ceremony

Boys like best the ceremony of thanksgiving for the renewal of life and the reappearance of the moon, which takes place several days after ROSH HODESH. It is an outdoor ceremony, held on a clear night and in full view of the moon.

First a prayer of thanks to God for arranging the world in such an orderly manner is chanted. Then the bright moon is greeted and good wishes for the future are exchanged. Three times all say in unison:

> Shalom aleichem — peace to you:
> Aleichem shalom — to you peace:
> Good omen and good luck to us and to all Israel, Amen.

The more enthusiastic dance as they chant these greetings and good wishes, the boys usually trying to outdo their elders. KIDDUSH HALEVANAH, or Sanctification of the Moon, is the name for this ceremony, still observed by thousands of Jews in all parts of the world.

New Customs

In Palestine schools, ROSH HODESH is celebrated with special assemblies and programs. They call this TEKES ROSH HODESH, or ROSH HODESH ceremony. In each classroom, important incidents of the preceding month are reviewed, and forthcoming events of the new month are discussed. More ambitious programs, consisting of appropriate songs, poems, and playlets, are presented in the auditorium.

For the month of KISLEV a school assembly program might include some of the following topics: Review of the important events of the preceding month; Armistice Day; recalling the completion of the Talmud, which occurred during this month; Dr. Chaim Weitzmann's birthday; purchase of the Huleh region in Galilee; and Hanukah.

At the conclusion of the program, an announcement is made of the amount of money contributed to the Jewish National Fund by each class, and how much is expected during the coming month. ROSH HODESH is therefore also KEREN KAYEMET day in Palestine schools. The boxes are opened and the sum collected is counted by the pupils.

Rosh Hodesh

Similar programs and activities are conducted by Hebrew schools in Poland, Lithuania, and other countries. American Jewish schools are also beginning to introduce this custom. In some community centers, ROSH HODESH is the occasion for club assemblies. Since some of the old ROSH HODESH customs are no longer observed as in former generations, Jews are introducing new ways of celebrating the event.

Chapter 4

THE HIGH HOLY DAYS

WHILE the other holidays commemorate great historical events, ROSH HASHANAH and YOM KIPPUR are religious occasions devoted to prayer and serious thought, when Jews take stock of their ideals and deeds. The customs and ceremonies, accordingly, are the kind which promote thoughts about religion and God and about relations with one's fellowmen. On the High Holy Days Jews strive to acquire new ideas and new hopes to face the year ahead.

THE SOLEMN SEASON

ROSH HASHANAH and YOM KIPPUR are the high points of a forty-day period, from the first of ELUL to YOM KIPPUR, devoted to prayer and thought. During their long history, Jews have found need for such a solemn period of contemplation, prayer, and self-examination.

Call of the Shofar

This solemn season is proclaimed on the first of the Hebrew month ELUL with the blowing of the SHOFAR in the synagogue after the morning service. Every day of that month, with the exception of Sabbaths, the SHOFAR blasts are repeated, reminding the people that great holy days are approaching and urging them to begin taking stock of themselves and their conduct. Pious Jews chant Psalms every morning, while many visit the cemetery during the month. On the Sabbath before ROSH HASHANAH, the rabbi's sermon usually deals with the holy days ahead, explaining their meaning and customs.

Selihot — Prayers of Forgiveness

That Saturday evening, after midnight, or at early dawn, the first SELIHOT service takes place in the synagogue. Men, women, and older children gather to recite special prayers of repentance and forgiveness. Some of the selections recall the hardships of exile, persecution, and martyrdom which Jews have endured. The SELIHOT service is repeated each night until ROSH HASHANAH. When the New Year falls on

46

Monday or Tuesday, the SELIHOT services begin a week before, always on a Saturday night.

The days before ROSH HASHANAH are busy ones for many people. Officers and active members of synagogues are engaged in assigning seats. The cantor and choir rehearse daily. The rabbi prepares his sermons. Jews who live in villages and small towns where there are no synagogues, arrange for the journey to the nearest Jewish community to attend Holy Day services. At home, too, the preparations are numerous, —house cleaning, shopping, buying new clothes, getting the MAHZOR ready, and sending greeting cards.

Shanah Tovah Cards

Exchanging of SHANAH TOVAH greeting cards, although a comparatively new custom, is widely observed. Cards are sent to relatives, friends, and teachers, to the rabbi, to business associates, and to community leaders. Some print personal cards, others buy them at a stationery store, while pupils in Jewish schools often make their own. Many families avail themselves of the local Jewish magazines and newspapers to extend greetings to their friends.

Erev Rosh Hashanah

Those who attend SELIHOT services on the morning preceding ROSH HASHANAH, enter into the spirit of the holy occasion early in the day. After the SELIHOT, and the morning service which follows, pious Jews remain for the HATARAT NEDARIM ceremony. If a person has made a vow or a resolution to himself but has been unable to carry it out, at this ceremony he makes public confession of his failure before three individuals; they respond by reading special prayers stating that he is forgiven. However, vows or

47

promises made to another person or to God cannot be nullified in this manner.

From the synagogues, many proceed to the cemetery to pray at the graves of relatives and sages. In Jerusalem, the custom is to visit the Wailing Wall. Very pious Jews fast from dawn to sunset.

ROSH HASHANAH EVE

The holy day is officially ushered in with the lighting of the candles by mother at sunset. The candles are ignited so that the New Year may begin with light and joy. In addition to the usual blessing, she also recites the SHEHEHEYANU benediction. The family proceeds to synagogue for the evening service. At the conclusion of the service, the traditional ROSH HASHANAH greeting is exchanged in a spirit of joy and hope:

LESHANAH TOVAH TIKATEV!
(May you be inscribed for a good year!)

Food Customs

When father returns home, greeting the family with LESHANAH TOVAH, the table is set for a festive meal. At the head of the table lie two HALLOT baked in the shape of a ladder, a bird, or a crown. The ladder reminds us that on ROSH HASHANAH men are judged: some are destined to climb and prosper; others to descend and suffer reverses. The bird is a symbol of mercy, for God has mercy even upon birds. The crown stands for the kingship of God, which ROSH HASHANAH emphasizes.

The meal begins with KIDDUSH, followed by the HAMOTZI benediction. As each person receives a slice of the HALLAH, he dips it into honey, saying, "May it be a good and sweet year." In some homes the custom is to dip an apple in honey. Fish, a favorite food among Jews, is sure to be on the menu. On this occasion, the fish symbolizes fruitfulness. Father is served the head, for on ROSH HASHANAH every one hopes to be "a head rather than a tail," a leader among his fellows. In some homes, the head of a sheep is served for the same reason, and also as a reminder of the sacrifice of Isaac. On the second night a new fruit, one not yet tasted that season, is served for the SHEHEHEYANU benediction.

THE MORNING SERVICE

The sanctity of ROSH HASHANAH is felt most at the morning service in the synagogues. The prayers make one feel and understand the significance of the day as only great poems can. The SHOFAR ceremony is an unforgettable experience to persons of every age. The reading of the Torah, the rabbi's sermon, and the special melodies all lend beauty and meaning to the service.

The High Holy Days prayerbook, or MAHZOR, contains prayers composed by great poets and sages over many centuries, and also includes selections from the Bible and Talmud. Many ROSH HASHANAH and YOM KIPPUR prayers, called PIYUTIM or hymns of praise, were composed by such distinguished Hebrew poets as Eliezer Kalir, Judah Halevi, and Solomon ibn Gabirol.

Judge, King, and Lawgiver

You may remember the famous verse in Isaiah: "For the Lord is our Judge, the Lord is our Lawgiver, the Lord is our King; He will save us." The most important prayers in the

New Year's liturgy stress these fundamental ideas of the Jewish religion. A section of the MUSAF is devoted to these three ideas. After each group of prayers the SHOFAR is sounded.

The first part, MALCHIYOT, speaks of God as King of the Universe, and of the day when He will be accepted as ruler of the whole world. In the second part, ZICHRONOT, God is described as remembering the world and all that exists upon it, and as the Creator who passes judgment upon man and his actions. The third group, known as SHOFAROT, contains prayers about Torah and Zion, for the SHOFAR is associated with both. God is the great Lawgiver who bestowed the Torah upon Israel to the sound of the SHOFAR; God is the great Redeemer who has promised to deliver the Jews from exile, restore them as a nation in Palestine, and bring peace and freedom to all mankind.

Unetaneh Tokef

The best known and most beautiful prayer in the MAHZOR is UNETANEH TOKEF, composed by Rabbi Amnon of Mayence in the Middle Ages. It is told that the local bishop tried over and over again to convert Rabbi Amnon to Christianity, and finally succeeded in extracting a promise from the rabbi that he would give him an answer within three days. But the moment Rabbi Amnon uttered the promise, he realized what a grave sin he had committed, and spent the three days in praying and fasting. When he was brought before the bishop, he asked that "his tongue which spoke falsehood be cut out." The bishop, instead, had his fingers and toes severed.

This happened several days before ROSH HASHANAH. When the holy day arrived, Rabbi Amnon was carried to the synagogue, with the severed toes and fingers lying beside him. After the KEDUSHAH, he requested permission to offer a special prayer, at the conclusion of which he died. Several days later, the story continues, he appeared in a dream to one of the great teachers of the day, taught him the prayer, and asked that copies be made and sent to every Jewish community in the world.

UNETANEH TOKEF is a great religious poem. It speaks in beautiful language of the greatness of God and the littleness of man, and how on ROSH HASHANAH man is judged. God is the great shepherd before whom all human beings pass for judgment on ROSH HASHANAH and YOM KIPPUR. On these days it is determined who may live and who shall die, who will prosper and who grow poor, who shall have rest and peace and who be destined to wander and suffer. Prayer, charity, and repentance can change an adverse verdict. For God does not want man to die but rather to correct his ways and live on. What is man? He comes from the dust and to dust he returns. He is like a fragile potsherd, a fleeting shadow, a dream that vanishes. But God is the living, everlasting King.

The Shofar Ceremony

The most impressive moment of the morning service is the SHOFAR ceremony. A sacred hush descends as everyone stands waiting for the notes of the hallowed instrument made from a ram's horn. Like the MENORAH, the SHOFAR is a holy symbol associated with important historical events, lofty ideals, and old-new hopes. Many of these associations flash through the mind of the Jew as he listens to the blasts.

He remembers the AKEDAH, the offering of Isaac by Abraham, for the AKEDAH has come to symbolize Israel's devotion

JEWISH HOLIDAYS AND FESTIVALS

to his faith and God. He recalls also how the children of
Israel received the Ten Commandments at Mount Sinai to
the accompaniment of SHOFAR blasts. He is reminded, furthermore, with sadness in the heart, of the destruction of the
holy Temple in Jerusalem, and how ever since then the
Jews have suffered exile and persecution. Above all, he recalls the promise of redemption—the return of the Jews to
Palestine and the establishment of everlasting peace and
good will in the world.

To Maimonides the call of the SHOFAR seemed to say:

> Awake, ye sleepers, and ponder your deeds; remem-
> ber your Creator and go back to Him in penitence. Be
> not of those who miss reality in their hunt after shad-
> ows, and waste their years in seeking after vain things
> which cannot profit or deliver. Look well to your souls
> and consider your acts; forsake each of you his evil
> ways and thoughts, and return to God, so that He
> may have mercy upon you.

The SHOFAR ceremony begins with the chanting of Psalm
37, which tells that God's sovereignty over all people will
some day be proclaimed with the blowing of the SHOFAR.
Seven times this beautiful poem is repeated. Then the
proper benedictions are recited and the horn is sounded.
The tones produced are called TEKIAH, SHEVARIM, and
TERUAH. TEKIAH is a long note; SHEVARIM consists of three
shorter notes; TERUAH is made up of nine quick, sharp calls.
These notes are repeated several times in different sequences.
A tradition explains that the three distinct notes are in
honor of the patriarchs, Abraham, Isaac, and Jacob. Blowing the SHOFAR has been part of the ROSH HASHANAH service
ever since ancient days.

THE HIGH HOLY DAYS

Reading the Torah

As on all holidays, reading from the Torah and from the Prophets is part of the ROSH HASHANAH service. The Torah selection on the first day is from Genesis XXI, where it is told how God remembered Sarah and blessed her with a son, Isaac. The HAFTORAH is from Samuel I, and narrates how Hannah's prayers were granted, so that she gave birth to Samuel. According to tradition, both Sarah's and Hannah's pleas were granted on ROSH HASHANAH. On the second day, the chapter in Genesis describing the AKEDAH is read from the Torah, while the HAFTORAH, from the Book of Jeremiah, foretells the return of the Jews to Palestine. The Torah selections are chanted with a special melody reserved for the High Holy Days.

Tashlich

After MINHAH (afternoon service), orthodox Jews attend the TASHLICH ceremony, which takes place on the bank of a river or near some other body of fresh water. Appropriate prayers are recited, and then each person shakes the corner of his garment to indicate that it is in man's power to shake himself free of sin and to correct his ways. The ceremony takes place near fresh water where fish thrive, because man is compared to fish. Just as fish are apt to be caught in a net, so man gets himself into trouble if he does not watch his conduct. Fish also symbolize fruitfulness and plenty.

ORIGIN AND MEANING OF ROSH HASHANAH

Our ancestors had several dates in the calendar which marked the beginning of important seasons of the year. The first of TISHRI was the beginning of the economic year. But the months were counted from NISAN, in the spring, rather than TISHRI. The reign of kings was also reckoned from the spring month. The fifteenth of SHEVAT was considered New Year's day for trees. The Talmud speaks of four dates when the world is judged: on PESACH for grains, on SHAVUOT for fruit, and on SUCCOT for water, while on ROSH HASHANAH man himself is judged.

In time, the first of Tishri became *the* Rosh Hashanah. Tishri marks the beginning of the rainy season in Palestine. And with the first rains the farmer goes out to plow and plant, and the year's work begins. Business transactions, sabbatical years, and jubilee years were all counted from the first of Tishri. The Bible, in commanding the observance of Rosh Hashanah, states, "In the seventh month, in the first day of the month, shall be a solemn rest unto you, a memorial proclaimed with the blast of horns, a holy convocation. . . ." Rosh Hashanah is observed two days in Palestine also.* Reform Jews keep only one day.

As time went on a great many important events came to be associated with this date: the creation of the world; the creation of Adam; the birth of Abraham, Isaac, Jacob, and Samuel; the day Joseph was freed from prison; and when the Hebrews ceased to be slaves in Egypt. Rosh Hashanah was also to be the great day of the future — when the Jewish people would be redeemed from exile and restored to their ancient homeland.

The Christian New Year

The ancient Egyptians, Phoenicians, Persians, and Greeks also observed the New Year in early autumn, and probably for the same reason as the Jews. The Romans, however, be-

---

* See Ch. 3, p. 37 f., why Rosh Hashanah and other holidays are observed two days, even though the Bible prescribes but one.

gan their year at the winter solstice on December 21, and from the time of Caesar on January 1. In medieval times, most Christian people celebrated the New Year on the 25th of March. The Gregorian calendar (1582) designated January 1 as the beginning of the year. While this date was at once accepted in Catholic lands, Germany, Denmark, Sweden, and England did not make the change until the 18th century. Christians celebrate New Year on January 1 in accordance with this tradition. They observe the day with merrymaking rather than in a serious mood, as do the Jews.

Four-Fold Meaning

Rosh Hashanah has a four-fold meaning. It is the New Year, the Day of Remembrance, the Day of Judgment, and the Day of Shofar Blowing. On Rosh Hashanah the Jew examines his thoughts and deeds of the past, and prays that God remember him kindly. For it is a Day of Judgment when man passes before the Creator and when his actions are evaluated. As a Day of Shofar Blowing, it is a time when the Jew reviews the history of his people and prays that the wandering of the Jews may soon come to an end and the Jewish people be restored in Palestine. Rosh Hashanah is also New Year's Day. The greeting cards, dipping of bread in honey, and the other customs are intended to express hope that the year ahead will bring joy and gladness to us personally, to all of Israel, and to the whole world.

BETWEEN ROSH HASHANAH AND YOM KIPPUR

The ten days from Rosh Hashanah to Yom Kippur, inclusive, are known as ASERET YEMEY TESHUVAH, or Ten Days of Penitence. According to tradition, an unfavorable verdict may be changed by repentance and charity. Each day the famous prayer of confession which begins "Our Father, our King" is recited at the service. In Palestine, pilgrimages are made to the tomb of Rachel and other sacred burial places, as well as to the graves of relatives. In other countries also it is customary to visit the cemetery. No weddings or banquets may be held during these days. Learned Jews read and study in the sacred books, and review the MAHZOR to be sure of the meaning of the prayers.

At the same time, the feeling which prevails is not one of sadness but of thoughtfulness and kindliness. The greeting exchanged during these days is GEMAR HATIMAH TOVAH, "May the final verdict be favorable."

Fast of Gedaliah

On the third of Tishri, the day after Rosh Hashanah, comes the Fast of Gedaliah. Gedaliah was a descendant of the royal house of David who was appointed governor of Palestine when the First Temple was destroyed by the Babylonians. With his appointment, hopes rose high among the Jews remaining in Palestine that after all this was not to be the end of their nation and independence. Unfortunately, Gedaliah was assassinated * and their high hopes were blasted. So heart-broken were the Jews that they declared the day of his death a fast, which Jews have observed ever since.

Shabbat Shuvah

As might be expected, the Sabbath between Rosh Hashanah and Yom Kippur is a special Sabbath, called SHABBAT SHUVAH or Sabbath of Penitence. The HAFTORAH is the

---

* Gedaliah is thought to have been assassinated on Rosh Hashanah, and the fast was observed on the next day.

famous chapter 14 from Hosea, in which the prophet calls out, "Return, O Israel, unto the Lord, your God!" The rabbi's sermon also deals with the subject of repentance.

EREV YOM KIPPUR

Erev Yom Kippur is a half-holiday, observed with prayers, ceremonies, and good food. It begins on the preceding evening with the KAPAROT ceremony. At dawn SELIHOT are said. Then follows the morning service, after which cakes are distributed to every one, in token of a good year. The solemn aspect of the day is emphasized in such customs as visiting the cemetery and receiving "thirty-nine lashes." Pious Jews ask a neighbor or friend to strike them thirty-nine times with a strap as self-inflicted punishment for sins committed.

The noon meal at home is festive; in view of the long fast ahead, one should eat well. Again fish is on the menu. Also, as on Rosh Hashanah, the HALLOT are baked in special shapes—a ladder, to express hope that the Yom Kippur prayers may reach heaven, or wings, because on Yom Kippur the Midrash compares man to the angels.

At the MINHAH service in the synagogue, everyone drops coins in the charity plates placed on a table at the entrance. ZEDAKAH, or charity, may save one from punishment and even death, according to traditional belief. Many bring large candles to the synagogue, which are lit in memory of dead parents. At home, mother lights candles as on all holidays.

Kaparot

The KAPAROT ceremony, performed usually on the night before Yom Kippur, is a very ancient custom, reminiscent of the animal sacrifices in Temple days. After the Temple was destroyed, prayers took the place of sacrifices. But for some reason the KAPAROT ceremony has persisted, even though many rabbis, among them the great Maimonides, were opposed to it. The ceremony consists of offering a rooster for a male and a hen for a female. As the person swings the fowl over his head, he reads several prayers which say, in effect: May this be a substitute for me; if it has been ordained that I die, may this fowl die in my place. The fowl or its value in money must be donated to charity. In most Jewish homes, money is used instead, which is contributed to a charitable cause.

Peace and Friendship

A significant custom is begging forgiveness of one another. Yom Kippur prayers and fasting atone only for sins committed against God and not for wrongs incurred towards fellowmen. These are not forgiven unless one makes up with the person wronged or offended. Persons not on speaking terms make peace with one another, the younger of the two usually taking the initiative. Enemies are expected to become friends; hatreds and wrongs are to be forgotten. Public spirited individuals take upon themselves the role of peace-makers on this day. Friends and relatives send cakes to one another as tokens of friendship. Thus Yom Kippur serves to promote friendship and good-will among men.

The Fast-Meal

The fast-meal must be eaten before sunset. After that no food or drink may be taken until after sunset the following day. Everyone is expected to fast, except children under

58

thirteen and sick persons. Fasting on Yom Kippur is meant not merely as self-inflicted punishment but also to prove to one's self that the body can abstain from the temptation of food for a day. Those who fast are more likely to think critically of themselves and to feel deeply the meaning of the confessions and prayers of the day. The meal is festal and plentiful. As on Rosh Hashanah, bread is dipped in honey. To prevent undue thirst, no highly seasoned foods are served.

"During the meal all sit silent and pensive. Words are few and uttered slowly and softly and with a peculiar tenderness. Every one is absorbed in thought. Fear and hope, doubt and confidence, are intermingled. One sits still and awaits the arrival of the greatest and most sacred day of the year, the great and solemn day when the judgment, the verdict of life and death, of health and disease, is to be rendered. Will the whole family sit together again and prepare for the fast?" *

Blessing the Children

Before leaving for the Kol Nidre service it is customary in many homes for the father to bless his children. This, too, is a very old Jewish custom, dating back to Abraham, Isaac, and Jacob. The blessing, freely translated, is as follows:

May God make you as Ephraim and Manasseh. May it be the will of our Father in heaven to implant within your heart love and fear of Him. May you desire to study the Torah and obey its commandments. May your eyes look straight ahead, your mouth speak the

* After A. S. Sachs, *Worlds that Passed*, p. 176.

truth, your hands perform good deeds, and your legs
be quick to do the will of God. May He grant you up-
right sons and daughters who will live in accordance
with the Torah. May your source of livelihood be secure, so that you will earn a living without depending
on the favors of man and have time to worship the
Lord. May you be inscribed for a long and happy life.

KOL NIDRE NIGHT

KOL NIDRE night is holy night. Only the SHOFAR ceremony on Rosh Hashanah may be compared to it in solem-
nity. Adults and children enter the synagogue as if on tip-
toe. The large candles seem to say that this is to be no ordi-
nary service. The men wear the TALLIT, while many are
robed in the white KITTEL, which stands for purity, joy,
and confidence, and at the same time is a reminder of
shrouds. The women, too, are dressed in white. Now the
ark is opened and the scrolls are taken out. The congregation stands up, eyes riveted on the BIMAH. The cantor begins to sing the famed KOL NIDRE prayer in the equally noted
and beautiful melody. Thrice he chants it, the congregation repeating the prayer each time.

The Kol Nidre Prayer

Kol Nidre is really a declaration rather than a prayer — a
declaration stating that all vows and obligations not carried
out are hereby voided and nullified. In the Middle Ages, it
often happened that Jews were compelled to assume obligations contrary to the Jewish religion. During the Inquisition
in Spain, for example, countless thousands were forced to
become Christians. Outwardly they vowed to live as Christians, but secretly they continued to observe the Jewish

customs. It is for vows such as these that the KOL NIDRE was primarily intended. Promises and responsibilities undertaken by a person under normal circumstances cannot be voided by reciting a prayer. They must be fulfilled. Enemies have often avowed that a Jew's promise is not worth anything, pointing to Kol Nidre as proof; but they are unaware of, or choose to ignore, the real intent of this prayer.

Confessions

Another very important prayer is the AL HET, or The Confessions. It enumerates many kinds of sin, since no one can be certain what sins he has committed or what is a sin and what is not. Dishonesty, cruelty, arrogance, gluttony, treachery, disrespect for parents, stubbornness, haughtiness — these and many others are included in the AL HET prayer, which is repeated eight times during Yom Kippur. Confession is the main theme of the Yom Kippur service, for the Jewish religion teaches that if a man sincerely repents or regrets his misdeeds, he will be forgiven. The confessions are all in the plural, for "All Jews are responsible for one another."

God and Man

A very beautiful prayer recited on KOL NIDRE night compares man to various kinds of materials and God to a master craftsman. God is the potter, man the clay; God the mason, man the stone; God the smith, man the pliable metal; God the captain, man the rudder; God the weaver, man the warp and woof. Following is the opening verse of this prayer:

61

JEWISH HOLIDAYS AND FESTIVALS

Lo! as the potter mouldeth plastic clay
To forms his varying fancy doth display,
So in Thy hand, O God of love, are we:
The bond* regard, let sin be veil'd from Thee.

Appeals for Funds

The rabbi's sermon has become an important part of the KOL NIDRE service. He speaks about the significance of the occasion, and, in most American synagogues, also makes an appeal for funds, either for the congregation itself or for some other worthy Jewish cause. KOL NIDRE night is the one time of the year when the largest number of Jews are to be found in synagogues and temples, and the opportunity is utilized to obtain necessary funds. Then, too, people feel generous on this occasion. No cash or checks, of course, are accepted; only the pledges are announced.

Yom Kippur Greetings

GEMAR HATIMAH TOVAH, may the final verdict be favorable, is the greeting exchanged after the service, as well as on Yom Kippur day. According to tradition, the verdict of every man, woman, and child is inscribed in the Book of Life on Rosh Hashanah and sealed on the Day of Atonement.

YOM KIPPUR DAY

Orthodox and conservative Jews spend the whole day in the synagogue, from early morning to after dark. Four distinct services take place on Yom Kippur day: SHAHARIT, MUSAF, MINHAH, and NEILAH. These constitute a large book, called the MAHZOR.

* The bond refers to the covenant between God and Israel.

THE HIGH HOLY DAYS

The liturgy of the day continues the mood of KOL NIDRE night, expressing similar sentiments and hopes. The spirit of confession and repentance prevails. The AL HET is repeated several times. The UNETANEH TOKEF is also recited. As on Rosh Hashanah, many of the selections are PIYUTIM, or poems of praise. Most of the PIYUTIM are based on the Hebrew alphabet, each verse beginning with a letter of the alphabet, in their fixed order. In some the name of the author is cleverly worked in.

With few exceptions, the prayers are in the plural. The Jew prays not only on his own behalf but also on behalf of his fellowmen. In the same spirit, some of the selections recall the suffering and martyrdom of Jews in the past and plead for forgiveness in their name. One such prayer tells the story of the Ten Martyrs executed by the Romans after the failure of the Bar Cochba revolt, among them the famous Rabbis Akiba and Simeon ben Gamaliel.* They were put to death because they continued to teach the Torah. Another prayer asks that God remember the covenant with Abraham, Isaac, and Jacob, the torture of slavery in Egypt, the great prophets, and the promise to restore the Jews to Palestine.

Reading from the Scriptures

Twice during the day the scrolls are taken out and read from. The portion from the Torah (Leviticus XV), read between SHAHARIT and MUSAF, prescribes the observance of Yom Kippur. Yom Kippur, the Bible states,

"shall be a statute forever unto you: in the seventh month, on the tenth day of the month, ye shall afflict

* See Ch. 10, pp. 155-59, for an account of the Bar Cochba revolt.

your souls, and shall do no manner of work, the home-born, or the stranger that sojourneth among you. For on this day shall atonement be made to cleanse you; from all your sins shall ye be cleansed before the Lord. It is a Sabbath of solemn rest unto you. . . ."

The HAFTORAH emphasizes the importance of good character and proper conduct. The kind of fast acceptable to God, says the prophet Isaiah, is one that leads man —

> To loose the fetters of wickedness,
> To undo the bonds of the yoke,
> And to let the oppressed go free,
> And that ye break every yoke.
>
> Isaiah, LVIII.

Equally significant is the HAFTORAH at the MINHAH service, which consists of the Book of Jonah. You remember that the prophet Jonah boarded a ship for a distant country "to flee . . . from the presence of the Lord." But he soon found that God was everywhere. This selection teaches that God is universal, and that His forgiving love extends to all peoples and all countries.

Memorial Service

A most solemn moment of the day takes place after the Scripture reading, when the memorial service is conducted. Remembering dear ones who are no longer alive brings tears to the eyes of everyone. It is customary to read the names of members or their relatives who have passed away during the year, and also of any others requested. In many congregations it is also the custom to offer a memorial prayer for Jews who have lost their lives because of persecution or in defense of Jewish communities. In recent years the brave Jewish defenders in Palestine have been thus included.

The Avodah

Part of the MUSAF is a description of the Temple ceremonies on Yom Kippur in ancient Jerusalem, called AVODAH or Sacred Service. For seven days preceding Yom Kippur, the high priest remained in the Temple studying, praying, and performing various rites, in preparation for the great event. The ceremonies began at dawn. Dressed in snow-white linen robes, he performed the rites of offering sacrifices and burning incense, once for himself, once for all the priests, and a third time on behalf of all the people. Each time he recited a prayer of confession, to which the priests and the people in the Temple responded by kneeling and chanting, "Blessed be His glorious sovereign name forever and ever." Thereupon he said to them, "Ye shall be clean," thus assuring the people that their sins would be forgiven.

Then followed the ceremony of sending the scapegoat into the wilderness, to symbolize the riddance of sins. Every one waited anxiously until the messenger returned and stated that the scapegoat had been dispatched in accordance with custom. Again sacrifices were offered and incense burned. At length came the loftiest moment of all, when the high priest entered the Holy of Holies, where no one but he could penetrate — once a year on Yom Kippur. The ceremony ended with more sacrifices and with chanting of psalms. The people, aglow with spiritual joy, had sought forgiveness and humbly believed it had been attained. They were happy, and expressed their thanksgiving in hymns of joy. The high priest was escorted home in a colorful procession in which thousands took part.

JEWISH HOLIDAYS AND FESTIVALS

The Vineyard Festival

In the vineyards of Jerusalem, as well as throughout Palestine, the people expressed their joy on Yom Kippur afternoon in another way. There the marriageable daughters and the eligible young men gathered to dance and sing. "Look up, young man, and choose wisely!" the girls called to the men. The poor borrowed clothes from the rich so that there would be no difference in dress between rich and poor, the aristocratic and the simple folk. Many happy marriages were concluded as a result of this festival. Indeed, it was considered so joyous an event that the Talmud states, "There were no happier days in Israel than . . . Yom Kippur."

Refreshment

As Yom Kippur continues in the synagogue, many begin to feel the effects of the fast. To refresh themselves, smelling salts, spirits of ammonia, and snuff tobacco are used. Among Oriental Jews spices and sprigs of mint are popular. Children are usually sure to supply themselves with these "refreshments." A new custom among some American Jews is that of sending flowers to their parents and friends in the synagogue.

NEILAH

The final service of the day, which is preceded by the MINHAH service, is appropriately called NEILAH, or closing. In ancient times, it evidently took place just before the Temple gates were closed. After a day of fasting and praying the worshippers are weary. But they gather strength for NEILAH, for the final appeal. An outsider would hardly be-

66

lieve that the men, women, and children before him had
been in the synagogue all day without food or drink, were
he to hear the ringing voice of the cantor and congregation
chanting:

> Open the gate for us,
> Yea, even at the closing of the gate,
> For the day is nearly past.
> The day is passing thus,
> The sun is low, the day is growing late.
> O let us come into Thy gates at last!

One of the last prayers ends with the word SALAHTI, "I
have forgiven." The Jew concludes Yom Kippur with confidence that he has been forgiven, that the day has helped
him to renew himself and strengthen his character, and
that the year ahead will be one of peace and goodness.

Hope and Confidence

At the very last, the KADDISH is recited, but is interrupted
for a minute by the SHOFAR — one long hopeful note. The
congregation calls out in unison three times, LESHANAH
HABAAH BIRUSHALAYIM, "Next year in Jerusalem!" Then
the cantor concludes the KADDISH. Yom Kippur is over.
The solemn season ends as it begins — with the sound of
the SHOFAR, symbolizing to the Jew the achievements and
struggles of the past, and the promise of happiness in the
future.

Yom Kippur is over, but the people, at least the men, are
not quite ready to go home. They remain for the MAARIV
service, which is chanted hurriedly, every one being hungry and anxious to depart. The HAVDALAH ceremony comes
next, since Yom Kippur is considered a Sabbath. Outside

the synagogue another ceremony awaits them — KIDDUSH HALEVANAH * performed outdoors. It is certainly appropriate to bless the new moon on the night after Yom Kippur, when Jews feel as if new-born. Before going home, good wishes for a happy and prosperous year are exchanged.

At Home

The home is cheerful and warm. On the table, light refreshments are waiting. At last the meal is served. Although every one is ravenously hungry, food is eaten sparingly. Incidents of the day are related at the table. Later friends and relatives come to visit and find out how the fasting has affected them. In some homes family parties are held. Jewish clubs, too, arrange parties for their members. The evening is spent merrily, continuing the spirit of confidence and hope which prevails at the conclusion of the Day of Atonement. As if to express their faith in a bright future, many Jews drive the first post of the Succah to be erected for the joyous festival of SUCCOT which is next on the calendar.

* See explanation and description of this ceremony in Ch. 3.

Chapter 5

SUCCOT AND SIMHAT TORAH

ON SUCCOT the Jew relives many heroic pages of Jewish history. He recalls the momentous journey to the Promised Land, the harvest in ancient Palestine, the sacred Temple in Jerusalem, and the role which the Torah has played in the history of the Jewish people. Now that Palestine is being rebuilt, Succot and its customs have even more meaning than in past generations.

"The Festival"

When the Jews lived as a nation in Palestine, Succot was the most important of all the festivals. Both the Bible and the Talmud refer to it as "The Festival."

So reads the Bible:

> "When you have gathered in the fruits of the land, ye shall keep the feast of the Lord seven days; on the first day shall be a solemn rest, and on the eighth day shall be a solemn rest, and ye shall take on the first day the fruits of goodly trees, branches of palm trees, and boughs of thick trees, and willows of the brook, and ye shall rejoice before the Lord your God seven days."
>
> Leviticus XXIII, 39-40.

Harvest Thanksgiving

Succot was thanksgiving week in ancient Palestine. Having completed the fruit harvest,* the people offered thanks in a joyous manner. They called the period HAG HAASIF, Festival of Ingathering. Being a religious people, they assembled for the celebrations at their places of worship. Samuel's father, Elkanah, came each year to Shiloh, the nearest sanctuary, to celebrate the harvest festival. Later, when sacrifices were permitted only in the Temple, Jerusalem became the one center of pilgrimage on all holidays.

At no other time was Jerusalem so crowded with pilgrims — now more so than on Pesach and Shavuot, the other pil-

---

* Shavuot marked the end of the grain harvesting season.

grimage festivals. We can picture the pilgrims on the happy journey to Jerusalem, bringing animals for sacrifice and fruits as gifts to the Temple, and carrying palm leaves and willow branches. We can also visualize the gay processions and ceremonies in the Temple, the Levites playing on harps and other instruments, and all chanting songs of thanksgiving. Among the multitudes were many from Babylon, Egypt, and other neighboring countries where Jewish communities existed.

Feast of Booths

In the same chapter of Leviticus describing observance of the festival we read: "Ye shall dwell in booths seven days ... that your generations may know that I made the children of Israel to dwell in booths when I brought them out of the land of Egypt."

The custom of the SUCCAH probably began among the exiles in Babylon. It served to recall to them not only the desert wanderings but also the booths in which the Jewish farmers lived during the harvest season in Palestine. They sat in their SUCCAHS and yearned for the homes and harvest booths of their fathers and grandfathers in Palestine. And so the festival came to be known also as HAG HASUCCOT or Feast of Tabernacles, and was celebrated as a national holiday to memorialize the journey from the land of slavery to the Promised Land.

The custom of booths was widely observed in Palestine, as well as in other countries where Jews lived. How they built the SUCCAH we are told in the Book of Nehemiah.

"Go forth unto the mount, and fetch olive branches, and branches of wild olive, and myrtle branches, and

palm branches, and branches of thick trees, to make
booths. . . . . So the people went forth, and brought
them, and made themselves booths, every one upon
the roof of his house, and in their courts, and in the
courts of the house of God, and in the broad places of
the water gate, and in the broad places of the gate of
Ephraim."

Nehemiah VIII, 15-16.

"The Season of Our Rejoicing"

New ceremonies were added to the festival as time went
on. Fortunately, we have descriptions of Temple Succot
celebrations in the Talmud, in the writings of Josephus and
in other works. It was now described also as ZEMAN
SIMHATENU, The Season of our Rejoicing.

A beautiful feature of the celebration was the daily procession with "the four species," the LULAV, myrtle, willow,
and ETROG. As the throngs of pilgrims marched around the
altar, they sang the HALLEL hymns and waved the palm
branches in unison. On the seventh day they marched
around seven times.

Simhat Bet Hashoevah

Even more splendid must have been the water-pouring
ceremony. It began early in the morning of the first day.
A golden pitcher was filled with water from the noted
Siloam spring outside the city. The carrier of the pitcher
was greeted at the Water Gate by three blasts of the shofar
and by shouts of joy from the tens of thousands of pilgrims.
Then the procession wound its way to the altar. The priest
took the golden vase and poured the water over the altar,
the Levites and pilgrims singing:

Succot and Simhat Torah

Ye shall draw water with joy
From the life-giving wells.

That night the Temple court was aglow with the light of many candelabra and torches. It was so bright that every courtyard in the city was illumined. Holding torches in their hands, pious learned men danced and sang around the pillars on which the candelabra were mounted. Then, at a given signal, the throng formed a huge procession and marched through the Court of Women to the eastern gate, while the levitical orchestra of harps, lutes, cymbals, and trumpets played appropriate melodies. The ceremony ended at the gate with the call repeated twice:

"We praise the Lord, upon Him are our eyes."

In Days to Come

So highly regarded was Succot in ancient times that the prophet Zechariah said: "And it shall come to pass that every one that is left of the nations . . . shall go up from year to year to worship the King, the Lord of hosts, and to keep the Feast of Tabernacles." The prophet is referring to messianic times, when all the nations of the world will live in peace and worship one God. That he mentions Succot as the holiday which all peoples of the world are to celebrate, indicates how important it was to our ancestors.

Succot in Modern Times

Succot has remained a major festival throughout the centuries. The ceremonies conducted in the Temple were transferred to the synagogue and to the home, with necessary changes, of course. Both the agricultural and historical meanings of the holiday were kept in mind. In time, new customs and prayers developed. The seventh day acquired a special name — HOSHANA RABBAH — while the ninth day became a special festival — Simhat Torah. In hundreds of communities today Succot is the most joyous festival in the Jewish calendar, even as it was in days of old.

In ancient times the Temple ceremonies were most important. Today the SUCCAH occupies the spotlight. Pains are taken to decorate it attractively with hangings, fruits, and flowers. Oriental Jews cover the walls with precious rugs. The roof of the SUCCAH is usually of pine-tree branches, but any green foliage may be used. The roofing is sparsely laid, so that the stars may be seen at night and the sunshine by day. Home SUCCAHS are built on roofs or in back yards. Sometimes porches are so constructed that the roofs can be replaced with green foliage for Succot. The most beautiful succahs are usually built by synagogues. In some Reform temples a small, decorative booth is erected on the pulpit.

The Succah as a Symbol

The SUCCAH recalls the pioneering days of the Jewish people. They were periods of hardship but evidently of high worth and importance, for again and again the prophets remind the people of those great days. In America, similarly, the frontier days are idealized. We speak with admiration of that era of heroism. We describe the life of the frontiersmen as one of freedom and self-reliance, simple and honest. The SUCCAH reminds us of the ideals of the pioneers and calls us to follow in their paths of honesty, love of freedom, self-reliance, and democracy.

Succot and Simhat Torah

The SUCCAH is also a reminder of the tents and shacks in which the HALUTZIM first live when they establish a new colony in Palestine, as well as of the harvest booths used by modern Jewish farmers in Eretz Yisrael. These pioneers, too, are idealists from whom we have much to learn.

For modern Jews the SUCCAH has even more associations than it had for our ancestors. It recalls not only the life in the desert and the harvest booths, but also twenty centuries of wandering over the wide world. Just as in the SUCCAH one does not feel safe from rain, wind, heat, and cold, so the Jews have never felt absolutely secure in any country. Today millions of Jews in Germany, Italy, Poland, Rumania, Hungary, and other countries are as unsafe as in any SUCCAH exposed to the elements.

Great teachers have pointed to the SUCCAH for lessons of conduct. Maimonides said it teaches us that in days of prosperity we should remember periods of evil and of poverty, so that we may remain humble and sincere at all times. The frail roof, the Talmud declares, should prevent us from putting our trust in the power of man.

Lulav and Etrog

The palm and citron occupy no less a place in Succot festivities today than in ancient times. To the LULAV are attached three myrtle twigs and two willow branches. Each of the first seven festival mornings except on the Sabbath the LULAV and ETROG are brought into the SUCCAH, where every member of the family pronounces a blessing over them, holding the LULAV in the right hand and the ETROG in the left. The palm leaf is shaken lightly after the benediction so that it rustles. One who has no ETROG and LULAV performs this ceremony in the synagogue, where they are also used in the daily procession around the BIMAH. To be the possessor of LULAV and ETROG is considered an honor. The ETROG must be without a blemish, shapely and of good color, while the LULAV should be tall and straight but flexible.

The LULAV and ETROG are also symbols of events and ideals. First of all, they represent harvest in Palestine and typify the trees of the country. Second, they recall the beautiful Temple ceremonies on "The Festival."

In the course of time new meanings have been read into "the four species." They stand for four important organs of the body: ETROG for the heart, LULAV for the spine, myrtle for the eye, and willow for the lips or mouth. How does each of these determine a person's character? Another interpretation compares them to four types of persons. The ETROG represents the person who has both beauty and character; the LULAV, one who is comely but has no character; the HADAS or myrtle, one who has character but lacks beauty; and the willow, one who lacks both.

Another meaning of the "four species" is that they symbolize four periods of Jewish history. The stately LULAV recalls the period of kings and prophets; the fragrant myrtle reminds us of the talmudic era of learning and wisdom; the drooping willow represents the centuries of exile and wandering; while the ETROG, both comely and fragrant, symbolizes hope for the future. Today the "four species" remind us as well of the new farm life of Jewish pioneers in Palestine.

First Two Days

Preparations for Succot are similar to those of other holidays, with the two notable exceptions of building the SUC- CAH and obtaining the LULAV and ETROG. Constructing the succah is a task for the whole family. Father and the boys do the building; mother and the girls are responsible for the decorations.

Before leaving for synagogue, mother lights the YOM TOV candles in the succah. Evening services in the BET HAKENESSET are brief, and the family is soon ready for the festive meal in the succah. As on all festivals, this begins with KIDDUSH. Then a song of welcome to Succot guests, called USHPIZIN, is sung. Seven guests are invited to the succah: Abraham, Isaac, Jacob, and Joseph; Moses and Aaron; and David. The HALLOT are in the shape of a ladder; the HAMOTZI is dipped in honey; fish, soup, and chicken are on the menu. Everything seems to taste different at this meal. Succot songs, as well as new Palestinian chants of soil and harvest, are sung between courses.

Procession with Lulav

The synagogue services on Succot are distinctive and colorful. After SHAHARIT, the HALLEL is chanted, LULAV and ETROG in hand. This prayer, you will remember, was sung in Temple days on Succot. After the MUSAF service, the ancient processional ceremony is enacted. The cantor goes first, then the rabbi, followed by all fortunate enough to have an ETROG and LULAV. But first the Holy Ark is opened. Round the BIMAH or down the aisles the procession marches. The hazan chants the HOSHANA prayer in the traditional melody, and the congregation recites it after him verse by verse. This ceremony is repeated each of the first seven days of the festival.

On both first and second days the readings from the Torah give an account of the holidays and festivals, includ-

ing Succot, and how they are to be observed.* The HAF-
TORAH on the first day is the chapter in Zechariah** where
the Feast of Tabernacles is mentioned as the one to be observed by all peoples of the world in messianic days. On
the second day, the HAFTORAH*** describes the dedication
of Solomon's Temple, which took place on Succot.

Simhat Bet Hashoevah

What of the ancient water-drawing festival which the
Talmud describes as the most impressive ceremony of all?
In many synagogues a special celebration is held on the
night of the second day. After the Psalm of Ascents is
chanted, the evening is spent in partaking of refreshments,
singing, and general entertainment. Jewish organizations
sometimes arrange special parties that evening, which they
call SIMHAT BET HASHOEVAH gatherings.

Hol Hamoed

The third, fourth, fifth, and sixth days are known as HOL
HAMOED, being only half-holidays. At home they are
observed with blessings over the LULAV and ETROG and by
eating in the SUCCAH. In the synagogue, the HALLEL prayers
are recited and the procession with the LULAV and the ETROG
is repeated daily. When one of the HOL HAMOED days happens to be Saturday, Ecclesiastes is read in the synagogue
silently by each person. Ecclesiastes or KOHELET is one of
the biblical books of wisdom.

HOL HAMOED is the time for community celebrations,
school entertainments, and club parties. Jewish schools ar-

* Leviticus XXII, 26-XXIII, 44.
** Zechariah XIV, 1-21.
*** I Kings VIII, 2-21.

range special assemblies which conclude with a visit to the
succah where the pupils are given fruit. Youth clubs hold
parties in a succah. In community centers and synagogues,
plays and concerts of Jewish interest are presented. In Palestine, it is a favorite time for hikes and overnight camping.

Hoshana Rabbah

The seventh day is more of a holiday than the rest of
hol hamoed. This is partly due to the tradition that the
season of judgment ends on this day rather than on Yom
Kippur. Pious Jews stay up part of the night chanting
psalms and reading Deuteronomy and other sacred books.
Many remain awake until after midnight, believing that the
heavens open then. Indeed, children have believed that if
one makes a wish at the moment the skies open, it is sure to
come true. The name of the day, hoshana rabbah, means
Great Help.

In the synagogue, pious men wear the kittel as on the
Day of Atonement. The procession with the lulav and
etrog is repeated seven times, and extra prayers are chanted.

In addition, willow branches, called hoshanot on this
occasion, are beaten after the service, to recall that in ancient times the altar in the Temple was decorated with
willow branches. This custom is also thought to symbolize
the renewal of life; the leaves of the willow fall off but new
ones will sprout next year. Another interesting explanation
connects this ceremony with the Babylonian captivity, as
told in one of the psalms:

> By the rivers of Babylon,
> There we sat down, yea, we wept,
> When we remembered Zion.

Upon the willows in the midst thereof
We hanged up our harps,
For there they that led us captive
    asked of us words of song
And our tormentors asked of us mirth:
'Sing us one of the songs of Zion.'
How shall we sing the Lord's song
In a foreign land?
If I forget thee, O Jerusalem,
Let my right hand forget her cunning.
Let my tongue cleave to the roof of my mouth,
If I remember thee not;
If I set not Jerusalem
Above my chiefest joy.
                Psalms CXXXVII.

This being the last day for ceremonial use of the LULAV, it is given to the children after the service. They enjoy weaving rings, bracelets, baskets, and similar articles from strips of the palm leaf.

Shemini Atzeret

The eighth day of Succot is in the nature of a separate festival. Eating in the SUCCAH is not obligatory, although commonly observed. The LULAV and ETROG are not used, and there is no processional in the synagogue. A more serious mood prevails in the house of worship, partly due to the memorial service before MUSAF. An important feature of the morning service is the prayer for rain, called simply GESHEM or Rain. Though away from Palestine, Jews in every part of the world have remembered to pray for rain in the ancient homeland at this season. Now that Palestine is being rebuilt, the prayer has immediate practical reasons. No work may be done on Shemini Atzeret, or Eighth Day of Solemn Assembly. The meal at home is festive. The afternoon is spent in visiting and receiving friends and relatives.

Simhat Torah

The last day of Succot is the jolliest. Originally it was the second day of Shemini Atzeret, but in time it became a new festival, a Torah Festival, which is what Simhat Torah means. It is one of the two Torah feasts, the other being Shavuot. On Shavuot Jews commemorate the great event on Mount Sinai when the ancient Hebrews received the Ten Commandments. Simhat Torah is the day when the reading of the Torah in the synagogue is concluded every year, and immediately after is resumed.

Reading from the Torah has been part of synagogue worship on the Sabbath, on the holidays, and on Mondays and Thursdays, since ancient times. Every Sabbath a SIDRAH or portion of the Torah is covered. In this way all of the HUMASH, or Five Books of Moses, is read through every year. On Simhat Torah the last chapter is completed and the first chapter in Genesis begun. Jews have been so happy in the Torah that Simhat Torah has remained the jolliest festival of the year, excepting Purim.

To enjoy the festival one should go to an old-fashioned hasidic SHUL on Simhat Torah eve and also the following morning. An unusual sight meets the eyes: men and women sit together, young folks chat and laugh merrily, children carry little flags. Only on Purim and Simhat Torah is such frolicking permitted.

Now the SHAMASH bangs on the table. But he is not the regular sexton, for on this night the honor of being master of ceremonies is bestowed upon a member of the congregation. He announces the first round of the ATA HARETA prayer, reading the first sentence himself, then treating his friends each to a verse. The congregation chants the verses after the readers. Seven times this prayer is repeated, so that practically every one has a turn to lead in chanting a passage.

The Hakafot

Next come the HAKAFOT, the processional with the Torah scrolls. All the scrolls are taken out. The rabbi, the GABBAI or president, and the other notables are honored first, each one being given a scroll to carry. The HAZAN advances in front chanting:

> Great and mighty, O help us!
> Kind and merciful, O help us!

The rest walk behind repeating the chant. In the rear of the march are the children with their flags. Everyone kisses the scrolls as they are carried by. Upon reaching the starting point in front of the ark, the marchers strike out singing and dancing. This is repeated as many times as may be necessary to give every one a turn to carry a scroll. Each round is concluded by singing and dancing. In the morning the HAKAFOT are repeated in the same manner.

Another Torah ceremony takes place at the morning service — reading the last and first chapters from the Torah. One man is chosen to be HATAN TORAH* and another one to be HATAN BERESHIT. The HATAN TORAH has the honor of

---

* Hatan means bridegroom.

calling up every one to the Torah for the reading of the last chapter in Deuteronomy, while the HATAN BERESHIT does the calling-up for the first chapter in Genesis. Everybody in the synagogue is called up twice, so as to have the MITZVAH of both concluding and commencing the Torah reading for the year. Even boys under thirteen, several together under a large TALLIT, are honored in this manner.

Dance and Be Merry

Nobody goes home to eat after the service. First there is a spread in the synagogue — wine, cakes, salted fish, and other refreshments. This is followed by dancing. The children are not forgotten, being given cakes, nuts, and fruit. From the synagogue they proceed to a member's house for more refreshments, song, and dance, then to another's home, then to a third and fourth. In this manner the whole afternoon and a goodly part of the evening are frolicked away.

Not all Jews celebrate Simhat Torah quite so merrily. In all orthodox and conservative synagogues, however, the ceremonies described above take place. The HAKAFOT processional is impressive everywhere, and the final and opening chapters of the Pentateuch are read. The afternoon and evening are spent gaily at home parties.

Succot in New Palestine

Nowhere in the world is Succot celebrated so joyously as in Palestine. The cities and colonies are studded with succahs. The booths of the Sephardic, Bucharan, and other Oriental Jews are richly decorated with rugs and hangings. Every morning, boys and men may be seen carrying the LULAV and ETROG to homes and synagogues. Plays, concerts, and lectures in honor of the festival are presented every evening. Among the youth, hiking and overnight camping are popular, and many spend the whole week seeing the country. If SUCCOT comes early in the season, vintage festivals are held in the grape-growing colonies. The traditional customs and ceremonies, of course, are widely observed.

An impressive event takes place in Jerusalem. Each year, on SUCCOT, the Jewish National Fund awards a banner to the school which has done most for the fund during the year. Hundreds of pupils from all parts of the country come to Jerusalem, in the spirit of ancient pilgrims, to take part in the celebration. The ceremony, on the grounds of the Keren Kayemet building, consists of flag drills, singing, responsive readings, and appropriate greetings by community leaders.

Small wonder that SUCCOT has occupied first place in the Jewish calendar as the most enjoyable of all festivals. Certainly in ancient days there was good reason for it. Our ancestors were an agricultural people. Soil, crops, and water meant bread and life to them. As a religious people, they looked to heaven for the bounties of nature and expressed thanksgiving with songs of praise to God and with ritual ceremonies. While offering thanks they at the same time prayed for a plentiful and happy future. Since the festival came after the harvest, when the people were free from field and orchard work, they could travel to Jerusalem for the celebrations.

Our ancestors loved their nation and country. Great events of the past were remembered for the lessons they taught and for the hopes and ideals they kept alive. Those years of desert wandering remained forever in the memories of the people. To be doubly sure of remembering this heroic period, they built huts or SUCCAHS and lived in them. Since the downfall of the Jewish state, Jews have continued to cherish the memory of the desert migrations, because they hoped that some day their wanderings would end at the gates of Palestine. This hope is being realized in our own day.

Chapter 6

HANUKAH, FESTIVAL OF LIGHTS

THE first HANUKAH in Jerusalem some twenty-one hundred years ago must have been a most joyous occasion. Had not the Jews in Palestine and those in other countries hoped against hope that Judah Maccabee and his followers would gain the victory? Now that Jerusalem was free and the Temple cleansed, they gathered in the thousands to celebrate and offer thanksgiving.

Not in three years, since Antiochus had set up a pagan altar in the Temple, had the holy sanctuary looked so clean and cheerful. For it had been the first task of the victorious soldiers, after entering Jerusalem, to cleanse and repair the Temple. Three weeks they labored. The Greek altar and idols were thrown out and a new altar was erected. The sacred objects which Antiochus had taken away were replaced with new ones. The forefront of the Temple was decorated with golden crowns and shields. Other curtains and veils were hung. Fresh loaves were baked and placed on the shew-bread table. A new MENORAH was made and illumined.

The First Hanukah Celebration

Most impressive must have been the scene when Judah Maccabee and the elders entered the Temple court to begin the ceremonies. The priests offered sacrifices and burned incense, while the Levites sang and played psalms of thanksgiving. So touched were the people that all prostrated themselves, praying that no more trouble come to them. Still chanting, they walked in procession with torches and palms in their hands as on SUCCOT. The harvest festival had not been observed that year, while the Temple was occupied by the Syrians. And so on this occasion they also celebrated the SUCCOT holiday. Throughout the country, wherever news of the victory had reached, the people probably gathered in SUCCAHS, synagogues, and public squares to express their happiness. Eight days the festivities continued, even as on SUCCOT.*

* The traditional explanation for Hanukah being celebrated eight days is that the pure oil in the miraculous little jug burned for that length of time.

HANUKAH, FESTIVAL OF LIGHTS

WHY HANUKAH?

Indeed, the Jews of the time, especially the Hasidim, had good reason to celebrate. For several generations the nation and its faith and culture had been gradually undermined. As a result of the conquest of Palestine by Alexander the Great a hundred and fifty years before, the Greek language, Greek gods and religious customs, as well as amphitheaters for games and sports, had been introduced into the country. These proved attractive to many Jews. They began to speak Greek instead of Hebrew. Young people spent their days in the gymnasiums. Some even began to adopt the religious customs of the Greeks, neglecting the Sabbath and the Jewish festivals. Greek rather than Hebrew names became common.

Hasidim and Hellenists

These Jews were called MITYAVNIM or Hellenists, and many of them seemed proud to be so known. Had Palestine been an independent country, the struggle against Hellenism would have been easier. But Palestine was now under the rule of Egypt, where Greek civilization predominated. The Egyptian kings appointed the important officials of Palestine, including the high priest and the tax collectors. Some officials, themselves Jews, were anxious to please their superiors and therefore promoted Hellenism in the land. One tax collector, Joseph ben Tobias, was especially active. Some wealthy Jews also sided with the Hellenists, for they had most to gain in the way of trade and commerce through friendly relationships with the rulers.

Greek civilization seemed to be a flood threatening to destroy everything the Jewish people held sacred—their

89

idea of one God, the Torah and prophetic teachings, the Sabbath and festivals, Temple and synagogue, the Hebrew language. Unless the flood was stemmed, the very existence of the people was in danger. All this was clearly realized by the devoted, patriotic Jews who called themselves HASIDIM. Other peoples, too, like the Syrians and the Egyptians, put up a struggle against Hellenism. But only the Jews were successful, perhaps because they treasured their own faith, language, and culture so deeply.

Civil War Breaks Out

Soon things came to a head. Palestine became part of the Syrian empire to the north, and was ruled by Antiochus Epiphanes when the active struggle began. Antiochus was an ambitious man. He wanted to build up an empire that would last, if he were to hold his own against Rome. In order to realize his ambition, he determined to mould all the peoples and tribes in this domain into one people with one language and one religion. And since he himself had been raised as a Greek, it was Greek civilization that was to become the cement for his united empire. Palestine was most important in that it lay between his country and Egypt.

Conditions in Palestine grew so bad that civil war was unavoidable. The Hellenists were now the rulers. So great was their power that the leader of the party, one named Jason, secured the high priesthood for himself by bribing Antiochus. Several years later, a more extreme Hellenist, Menelaus, outbid Jason and had himself appointed high priest, even though he was not of any priestly family. This bargaining for the holiest office in the Temple angered the people greatly. When rumors spread that Antiochus had been defeated in war, Jason returned from hiding and led his followers against Menelaus. Thus civil war broke out.

The Jewish Religion is Forbidden

The rumors proved false. Antiochus, having heard of the rebellion against Menelaus, unexpectedly attacked Jerusalem and inflicted severe punishment upon its inhabitants. Menelaus was returned to power. Then followed a period of oppression and suffering. Antiochus was determined to subdue Palestine by wiping out the Jewish religion and culture. The Temple was converted into a place of worship to Zeus, the dominant Greek god. Observance of the Sabbath, the dietary laws, and other religious customs and laws was forbidden. Both the Jewish nation and faith were in danger of extinction.

At first the Jews resisted bravely but passively. Hannah and her seven sons chose death in preference to worship of Greek idols. An old man, Eliezer, gave his life rather than mislead his people. Several thousand men, women, and children hiding in a cave, met death by suffocation to avoid breaking the Sabbath.

The Successful Revolt

As the oppression continued it became evident that the bravery exemplified by Hannah and her sons would not save the nation and its faith. Another kind of bravery was needed. Soon the call to action came, from Modin, a small village in which lived the Hasmonean family. Mattathias and his five sons raised the banner of revolt with the words: MI LADONAI ELAI! "Whoever is for the Lord, follow me!" Many answered the call and the war for independence began.

At first, being outnumbered by the Syrian army, they could carry on only guerrilla warfare. But as the Jewish forces increased, they began to fight in the open, under the courageous leadership of Judah Maccabee and his four brothers, Johanan, Simon, Jonathan, and Eliezer. News of the first victories spread throughout the country, and thousands of Hasidim found their way into Judah's camp. Before long he commanded a small but well trained army. Antiochus, who did not take the revolt seriously until his soldiers had suffered several defeats, sent three large armies to suppress the rebellion at one stroke. A decisive battle was fought at Emmaus. Vast courage and clever military tactics enabled the Jews to gain a victory over these greatly superior forces. Thus they cleared the way to Jerusalem, where Judah now proceeded to reestablish an independent Jewish government.

It was this victory that the Jews celebrated on that first HANUKAH. We today, however, know that Judah's first successes and the rededication of the Temple did not mark the end of the revolt. We recall on HANUKAH what followed: how for another generation the struggle for independence was waged bravely against a mighty empire. When Judah lost his life in a subsequent battle, Jonathan took his place and further strengthened the country. He was succeeded by Simon, under whose rule Palestine finally regained its independence.

WHAT HAPPENED TO HANUKAH

In the following decades HANUKAH must have been celebrated as a great festival. But a time came, only several generations later, when even famous teachers like Hillel and

Shammai were not quite certain how it was to be observed. Just why this should have happened to so important a holiday no one knows surely. Perhaps the opposition to the later Hasmoneans accounted for it. Or perhaps because the Books of the Maccabees, which contain the story of HANUKAH, were not widely known.

Books of the Maccabees

We have today four Books of the Maccabees, but only two of them are important. Maccabees I, written soon after the successful revolt, tells in detail the events which led up to the war for independence and describes the bravery of Mattathias, Judah, Jonathan, and Simon. It also contains speeches delivered by Mattathias and later by Judah to their loyal followers. The book was originally composed in Hebrew and then translated into Greek. Unfortunately the Hebrew version was lost and only the Greek remained. Maccabees II, first written in Greek, contains many of the HANUKAH stories and legends. Today we have good Hebrew and English translations of these books.

The Miracle of the Flask of Oil

Perhaps because the Books of the Maccabees were in Greek, the heroic story of HANUKAH was not well known when the Talmud was written down, for the only important reference to HANUKAH in the Talmud is the following question and answer:

What is Hanukah?

When the Hasmoneans overcame the Syrians and repaired the Temple, they found there only one flask

JEWISH HOLIDAYS AND FESTIVALS

of oil bearing the seal of the high priest. It contained
oil for only one day but a miracle happened and the oil
burned for eight days. Next year an eight-day festival
was declared, to be celebrated with songs of praise
and thanksgiving, for all times.

In the seventh century, a special MIDRASH, called MEGIL-
LAT ANTIOCHUS, was composed and read on HANUKAH, but
it too, does not tell the history of the Maccabees in full.

HANUKAH IN OLDEN TIMES

Nevertheless, HANUKAH remained a festive week in the
Jewish calendar, yielding second place only to PURIM
among the minor festivals. It was primarily a home holiday.
As time went on, new customs developed and special prayers and songs were composed. We may pay an imaginary
HANUKAH visit to a Jewish community a hundred years ago
or more.

Greetings and Lights

If we were in Venice we could not miss the HANUKAH
spirit upon entering the Jewish district. The canals are
swarming with gondolas, crowded with happy young folks.
They stop at every house illuminated with HANUKAH lights
to extend holiday greetings in joyous Hebrew songs. From
each house, greetings and good wishes are returned to the
merry gondoliers. The ghetto is bright with lights as at no
other time of the year. HANUKAH lamps twinkle on thresh-
olds and window sills.

In the Synagogue

Let us enter the synagogue, beautifully illumined, thanks
to the special society of young men who see that the syna-

gogue is cheerfully lighted on every joyous occasion. The service itself is not different from the daily evening service, with the exception of the HANUKAH light ceremony and the AL HANISIM prayer. Every heart beats a little faster when the prayer is chanted.

> We thank Thee for the miracles, the redemption, the mighty deeds and saving acts, as well as for the wars which Thou waged for our fathers in the days of old, at this season. In the days of the Hasmoneans, Mattathias son of Johanan the high priest and his five sons. . . . Thou delivered the strong into the hands of the weak, the many into the hands of the few . . . and the arrogant into the hands of those who occupied themselves with Thy Torah. . . . Thy children came into Thy sacred house, cleansed Thy Temple, purified Thy sanctuary, kindled lights in Thy holy courts, and appointed these eight days of Hanukah to give thanks and praises to Thy great name.

The Ceremony at Home

Let us spend the rest of the evening in a home. Father and sons are back from synagogue. Mother has long finished her chores, since it is customary not to do any work after the HANUKIYAH or HANUKAH lamp is lighted. The lamp, made of copper and decorated with designs of lions, vines, pomegranates, eagles, and other favorite Jewish symbols, rests on the window sill. The family gathers around the MENORAH while father pours in the oil. He recites the benedictions as he lights each wick, the family answering Amen. Then all chant in chorus the hymns HANEROT HALALU, and MAOZ

95

TZUR. It is the fifth night, but he kindles six lights, including the SHAMASH.*

Story of Judith

Now we join the family at the table for a delicious dairy meal in which cheese is most prominent. But why cheese and other dairy dishes? Because of brave Judith, whose courage delivered her community from death. Father tells them the story, which is associated with HANUKAH. Judith lived in Bethulia. The city was besieged by a large army commanded by Holofernes. When the food began to give out, the people lost all hope of saving their lives. Judith was a beautiful woman, and she decided to risk her own life in a bold attempt to rescue her people. Stealing out of the city, she somehow managed to obtain an interview with Holofernes. He was so charmed with her beauty that he suspected nothing. She entertained him, gave him *cheese* cakes to eat and plenty of wine. When he became drunk, she decapitated him, and brought the head back in a sack. Their commander dead, the enemy lost courage and fled before the Jews. Thus Judith delivered the city.

The Greatest Miracle

As the meal proceeds, other stories are recalled for the sake of the younger children, including the well-known tales of Hannah and her seven sons, the old man Eliezer, and the miraculous jug of oil. Father explains that this miracle of oil which burned for eight days is connected with the great miracle of the Jewish people, who have lived on

---

* The extra light, called *Shamash*, father explains, is because we are allowed only to see the Hanukah lights but not to use them. But this is hardly possible when the lamp is so close to us. By having an extra light it is as though we are benefiting from this additional light only and not from the others.

HANUKAH, FESTIVAL OF LIGHTS

and on for so many centuries in spite of continuous wandering and persecution, and are still alive today.

Other Hanukahs

One of the boys who is in his first year at the YESHIVAH tells them of other HANUKAHS or dedication festivals he has recently studied about: the HANUKAH celebration when the Tent of Meeting was completed in the days of Moses; the dedication of Solomon's Temple; the celebration when the Second Temple was opened; and the festival when Nehemiah finished building the walls of Jerusalem. We also remember these important events in the history of the Jewish people on HANUKAH.

Gifts and Games

Soon the meal is over. The school children are approaching father and whispering something in his ear. Smiling, he fetches his purse and hands each one several coins—HANUKAH GELT. But it is not for themselves. Tomorrow they will bring the money as a HANUKAH gift to their teacher. Father has ready a special present which he will deliver personally, a gift for the older daughter's future husband. Poor children receive HANUKAH GELT from the community chest.

The table having been cleared away, the family seat themselves for an evening of HANUKAH games. Two are playing KATOWES, a game of arithmetic riddles and puzzles. The answer to each one must be forty-four, which is the total number of lights on the eight days. The younger children are playing TRENDEL or DREIDEL. This is a four-winged spinning top with the four Hebrew letters—NUN, GIMEL, HEI, and SHIN. They stand for NES GADOL HAYAH SHAM, "A great miracle happened there." The older folks are playing cards. HANUKAH was one time when cards were permitted.

The games are frequently interrupted by knocks on the door. Most of the knockers are beggars who have come for their HANUKAH gifts. Generally, begging from door to door was not allowed by Jewish communities in those days; but HANUKAH was made an exception. Some of the visitors are relatives and friends who have come to spend the evening.

School Banquets

At one point a rather loud knock is heard, followed by equally loud song. The door opens and a half dozen boys troop in singing, "Buy us a little bread!" No one is surprised. HANUKAH is review time in the schools, and as a reward for hard work are not the pupils entitled to a feast? These boys are one of the several committees making the rounds from house to house to collect food and sweets for the banquet. Mother has been expecting the visit and she has a basket all packed for them.

Among the Yemenites

Were we to choose Oriental Jewish communities for our imaginary visit, we should find other HANUKAH customs. Among the Yemenites in Southern Arabia, we should hear in the synagogue the reading of MEGILLAT ANTIOCHUS or Scroll of Antiochus. If we were lucky, we might get an invitation to a children's HANUKAH party. Each child brings his refreshments with him—roasted corn, carrots, grape juice, and the like. Seated around the lighted HANUKIYAH, they eat, sing, and make merry. After the party, they form in line and march noisily through the streets, stopping to extend festival greetings at each house. Widows who have no grown sons invite them to come in. The youngsters need no second invitation. In they troop, perform the light ceremony for the women, and burst out singing and dancing.

HANUKAH TODAY

Most of the customs observed on HANUKAH a hundred and more years ago are with us today. We light the HANUKIYAH each of the eight days, beginning with one light on the first night and concluding with eight on the last. DREIDEL games are universally popular, as are card games and, more rarely, the clever KATOWES riddles. Children receive HANUKAH GELT, part of which they give to some worthy cause. Dairy dishes, including LATKES or pancakes, are eaten. In the synagogue, the AL HANISIM and the HALLEL prayers are recited. Among Yemenite Jews and Sephardim, the Antiochus MEGILLAH is read. In some communities, boys still collect food for school banquets.

However, while formerly HANUKAH was primarily a home festival, today it has become also a community holiday, celebrated with plays, entertainments, concerts, and parties. Some institutions display large MENORAHS in the lobby. Youth clubs hold HANUKAH parties and present plays. Thousands of young men and women go out on HANUKAH Sunday with Jewish National Fund boxes and flags to collect money for buying land in Palestine.

HANUKAH IN PALESTINE

In Palestine, HANUKAH is truly a Festival of Lights. In every village and colony, a large electric MENORAH, mounted on the water tower, illumines the settlement each night. In Tel Aviv, Jerusalem, and other cities, huge HANUKIYAHS are lighted on synagogues, schools, and other public buildings. Window displays in stores and shops are decorated with holiday designs. Small HANUKIYAHS twinkle from the window sill of every home.

Lighting the public HANUKIYAH is a picturesque and impressive ceremony in the cooperative colonies. The whole settlement, from toddling two-year-olds to graybeards, gathers around the water tower after dark. Their heads raised, eyes directed to the HANUKIYAH on the tower, the ceremony begins with an appropriate song by the children. From above rings out the clear voice of a child reciting the benediction. Amen! respond the people below. In a flash, the bright lights are on, and the crowd sings MAOZ TZUR. Then a procession is formed, first the nursery and kindergarten children, next elementary school pupils, after them the older boys and girls, and behind them the adults. Several carry torches. Singing HANUKAH melodies and new songs of bravery and freedom, they march to the schoolhouse to witness a program by the children and to partake of refreshments.

Ceremony and Parade in Tel Aviv

Even more picturesque is the public ceremony in Tel Aviv. At sunset the high school students as well as older pupils from the elementary schools assemble in a public square or in front of a synagogue. Every boy and girl carries a candle, while many have torches ready. They arrange themselves in a huge semi-circle, facing a decorated platform reserved for the mayor and other prominent citizens.

Hanukah, Festival of Lights

A large HANUKIYAH stands on the platform. All around the children are thousands of spectators.

The ceremony begins at dusk. The HAZAN walks up to the MENORAH and, chanting the benedictions, lights one candle after another. A loud chorus of Amen rings out from the thousands of pupils. The moment the HAZAN begins to kindle the HANUKIYAH, the children begin to light their own candles and torches. After a minute or two, the square becomes a sea of twinkling lights. A band strikes up the MAOZ TZUR and the thousands of children and guests join in one mighty chorus. Then the mayor extends the city's greetings, and a teacher speaks briefly about the significance of the festival. Again the band plays and the huge audience sings.

At a given signal, the twinkling lights and flaring torches begin to move—first one school, then a second, then a third, the band playing all the while. No, the children are not disbanding for home; they are forming in line for the annual HANUKAH parade. Up one street and down the next they march, the lighted candles in their hands. The little lights dance up and down as they are raised and lowered with every step. Ten thousand young voices sing lustily. All along the route, the sidewalks are crowded with thousands of spectators.

A more adventurous HANUKAH custom in Palestine is hiking to Modin, ancient home of the Hasmoneans, where the banner of revolt was raised by Mattathias and his five sons. There are now caves and tombs where the Hasmoneans are said to have been buried. Young Jews from all parts of the country come to Modin on HANUKAH to pay their respects to the brave leaders who served their nation and religion so faithfully.

Jewish Holidays and Festivals

The Meaning of Hanukah

Not in twenty centuries has HANUKAH been so important a festival as it has become in our own day. No less than Jews in the past, we today read in the little lights the story of eternal Israel. We understand a little better, perhaps, what it means to enjoy liberty and to have heroes and heroines. We also realize what it means to have Hellenists. Today we call them assimilationists—Jews who do not care whether the holidays and customs are observed, whether the Hebrew language, the Bible, and Jewish history are studied, whether Palestine is rebuilt, whether the Jewish community is well organized, whether, in fact, the Jewish people and the Jewish religion survive or not. HANUKAH, each year, reminds us of the conflict between the Hasidim and Hellenists of old and inspires us to wage a peaceful battle against assimilation.

We know, too, how dearly Jews are paying the price of being Jews. In Germany, Italy, Poland, Hungary, and other countries Jews are persecuted for no other reason than their origin. In democratic countries, including America, Jews are discriminated against in many ways. The poison of Nazism and Fascism is spreading. Once again mighty powers are determined to destroy the Jewish people and Judaism. HANUKAH comes each year and bids us have courage and hope. More than that, it teaches us that we can save ourselves only by banding together to fight the menace.

But there is another reason why HANUKAH has become so important a holiday—the rebuilding of Palestine. When the early Zionists and the first HALUTZIM read how a handful of Jews in the time of the Maccabees achieved what seemed an impossible task, they were inspired to say, "It can and will be done again!" Zionist clubs began to arrange mass meetings and concerts during HANUKAH week. Hebrew schools presented plays depicting the bravery of Judah Maccabee and the Hasidim. Synagogues and community centers followed suit. Soon reports of the picturesque ceremonies in Tel Aviv and in the colonies spread widely. The message of HANUKAH encourages us to hope that Eretz Yisrael may once again become the center of the Jewish people and Jewish culture even as after the Maccabean victories.

Chapter 7

HAMISHAH ASAR BISHEVAT

SHEVAT, the Hebrew month approximating February, marks the beginning of spring in Palestine. From December to February it rains heavily and rather steadily, with occasional storms. All vegetation is at a standstill, dormant, as if Mother Nature were asleep. With the exception of the olive, the cypress, the carob, and the pine, the trees are bare of leaves. The meadows, while green with grass, lack the luster of spring. In the newly-ploughed and sown fields, the first shoots are raising their little weak heads from the furrows.

With the first mild days of SHEVAT, nature begins to clothe itself in spring garb. Blood-red poppies or anemones sprout in every meadow and on mountain sides. From crevices in the rocky slopes, cyclamens peep out. Trees, too, begin to blossom. The almond, named SHAKED, the quick one, is the first to open its buds. As if overnight, every almond tree stands bedecked with rose-white flowers. Nature has awakened from its slumber. Spring brings many new arrivals among the birds. Some have come to stay in Palestine, while others are on flight to more northern countries.

Love of Trees

Being an agricultural people, the ancient Jews lived close to nature. They particularly loved trees and treasured them for their fruit, shade, and other uses. Happy is the wise and righteous man, we read in the Psalms, "and he shall be like a tree planted by the streams of water, that brings forth its fruit in its season, and whose leaf shall not wither." While yet in the desert they were commanded, "And when ye shall come into the land (Palestine), ye shall plant all manner of trees." When a city is conquered, the Bible states, "Ye shall not destroy its trees . . . for the trees of the field are meant for man."

The Talmud and Midrash are equally emphatic about their value. "Man's life depends on the tree," we read in one book. "All the trees were created for the use and enjoyment of living beings," is stated elsewhere. "It is forbidden to live in a city which has no gardens and greens." The Torah, you will remember, is compared to a tree: "For it is a tree of life." Often certain trees were spoken of as representing human characteristics:—the cedar as a symbol of courage and strength; the olive, of wisdom; the grapevine, of joy and childbearing; and the palm, of beauty and stateliness.

Small wonder that one day a year was set aside as ROSH HASHANAH LEILANOT, or New Year of the Trees, the day when trees are judged:—which are destined to flourish and grow tall and which to wither and shrink; which to suffer from lightning, winds, and insects, and which to withstand all danger. At one time it seems to have been observed on the first of SHEVAT in the valleys and plains, and two weeks later in hilly country, since in the lower regions the trees begin to bloom a little earlier. Later, the fifteenth of SHEVAT was adopted for the entire country.

Trees for Children

A beautiful, and at the same time practical, custom was observed in ancient Palestine on HAMISHAH ASAR. A tree was planted upon the birth of a child—a cedar sapling for each boy born that year and cypress for a girl. When the children married, branches of these trees were used for the HUPPAH or bridal canopy. In this manner, trees were associated with two of the most important events in a person's life, birth and marriage. Children grew up with a love for trees. Moreover, this custom served to keep the country wooded from generation to generation.

Date for the Tithe

The fifteenth of SHEVAT was a red-letter day in the ancient Jewish calendar also in connection with the tithe. The tithe was the agricultural impost; it provided that farmers give a tenth of their produce to the government as income tax. After HAMISHAH ASAR, it was prohibited to use for the tithe products harvested prior to that date.

WHY HAMISHAH ASAR SURVIVED

As a nature festival without religious ceremonies, HAMISHAH ASAR should have been forgotten after the Jews were torn from Palestine. That it lived on shows how deep was the longing of the Jews for Palestine. Even in countries where severe frost and snow reign during SHEVAT, Jews have continued to celebrate HAMISHAH ASAR each year, to this very day.

Think of the Jew in the ghetto. Neither he nor his fathers for centuries had lived on the soil. The crowded Jewish district was often bare of trees and shrubs. Perhaps because he was deprived of nature and farm life, he longed for them all the more. On HAMISHAH ASAR he would imagine himself walking in the verdant fields and orchards of Palestine, hoping all the while that some day the homeland would be rebuilt and Jews would again plant trees and eat their fruits.

In the winter people long for spring, especially in the cold northern countries. HAMISHAH ASAR has served as a harbinger of spring to the Jew, in whatever country he has lived. Another month, and it will begin to thaw. No more biting frosts and furious snow storms. How good it will be when the sun smiles again warmly! Perhaps with milder days will come better times for the Jewish people.

A Children's Holiday

In European countries, HAMISHAH ASAR was primarily a school holiday. Each pupil would bring figs, dates, raisins, almonds, BOKSER or St. John's bread, and other fruits native to Palestine. The teacher would collect all the fruit and divide it equally among the boys, so that there be no distinction between rich and poor. The children would recite the benedictions in chorus and eat the fruit, while the teacher told them stories about Palestine, and read passages from the Bible and Talmud about trees and their importance to human life. Later that day, the children ate more fruit at home.

Commencement Day

HAMISHAH ASAR was the day when the first school term ended and the second began. If a certain grade was ready to commence a new book of the Bible or the Talmud, the formal beginning would be made on HAMISHAH ASAR. Likewise, the formal completion of a chapter or a book would be arranged for this day. On such occasions, the parents came to school to share with their children the joy of passing to the study of a more advanced work. They brought fruit, ginger cakes, and BOKSER for children and teacher.

Oriental Customs

HAMISHAH ASAR has been, and still is, more widely observed among oriental Jews than in Western countries, perhaps because the climate and fruit of the countries where they have lived are similar to those of Palestine. In fact, the Sephardic Jews have compiled a special book for the festival, called PERI ETZ HADAR, or Fruit of the Citrus Tree. It contains selections from the ZOHAR and other sacred books about Palestine and its natural products.

Moroccan Jews celebrate HAMISHAH ASAR eve with a banquet at the synagogue, immediately after the MAARIV service. Seated at long tables, the guests are served fruit by the officers of the synagogue. The honor of reciting the SHEHEHEYANU benediction is accorded to the oldest man present, while the other BERACHOT, one for each variety of fruit, are chanted by all the guests. After each benediction, appropriate selections from the Fruit of the Citrus Tree are read and explained by the HAHAM, as their rabbi is called.

At home, the family is waiting anxiously for father to return from the synagogue. Soon he is back and the feast begins. Fruits are generously passed around to every one. While eating, the father answers questions about HAMISHAH ASAR.

On the morrow, the younger children make the rounds of all the relatives, grandfather and grandmother, uncles and aunts, and more distant kin. Everywhere, they are welcomed and given fruits, which they put into little sacks their mother has provided. The children move rather quickly from house to house, to see who will obtain the largest amount of fruit in the shortest time.

Other oriental Jews celebrate HAMISHAH ASAR in an equally festive manner. The men, rather than the women, shop for the fruit. Everyone buys generously; even the poor do not spare their pennies for HAMISHAH ASAR fruit. The rich hold parties and banquets at their homes, to which children are invited, to entertain the guests with songs. Picnics, too, are not unknown in the warm oriental countries on HAMISHAH ASAR.

THE NEW HAMISHAH ASAR

The HAMISHAH ASAR customs described may be witnessed today in a thousand Jewish communities. But today the old customs have new meaning. The trees of Palestine are no longer things to remember. They are living objects to be planted by sturdy pioneers, for during the many centuries that Jews were away from Palestine, the country was denuded of trees and shrubs. The forests seen in Palestine today were planted in recent years by Jewish pioneers.

Why Trees?

Trees play an important role in the plan of upbuilding Palestine. They are necessary for the beauty of the country, and for the fruits they bear; for shade and shelter to man, beast, and bird; for lumber to build homes and make furniture; for protection from winds and storms; for prevention of soil erosion; and, most important, for draining the malaria-breeding swamps.

In Palestine, therefore, HAMISHAH ASAR* is devoted to planting trees, and since it has always been a children's festival, the privilege is accorded to them. Then, too, as the farmers and workers of tomorrow, the children must be imbued with a strong attachment to their country. A child who plants a tree with his own hands unites himself lastingly with the soil upon which it grows. Following is a description of the planting ceremony in Tel Aviv in 1937. Similar celebrations, combining festivity with useful labor, are carried out in every city and colony in Palestine.

Planting in Tel Aviv

"The Planting Ceremony this year (1937) proved to be a most impressive and significant children's folk festival. The spot was well chosen—a green field adjoining verdant Sa-

---

* Palestinians usually call the holiday *T'u Bishevat*. *T'u* stands for the Hebrew letters *Tet* and *Vav*, which have a numerical value of fifteen.

rona, with the hillocks and gardens of Ramat Gan for immediate background, and the distant Hills of Judea for a backdrop. This spot was selected not only for its natural setting, but also because it adjoins Bialik Boulevard, where the planting was to take place.

"The ceremony began, after the opening bugle-call, with the march of the planters. As the band struck up, a thousand sturdy sixth-grade pupils from the Tel Aviv schools poured into the field in orderly, colorful files. Each child had a green wreath on his head, while every class carried an appropriate banner. One banner read, 'The desert shall yet bloom'; another, 'They cut down sycamores, we shall plant cedars in their stead.' One class carried a huge sketch of an apartment building surrounded by trees and flowers. Alongside was an inscription, 'One may not live in a house which has no flower garden.'

"Then five comely youths in priestly garb ascended the simple but effective platform. From a scroll they read in unison the proclamation of the day:

'The fifteenth day of the eleventh month shall be a day of planting unto you. Every tree, flower, and plant shall be remembered on that day. And it shall be when thou art come to the Land, thou shalt plant every variety of tree. And thou shalt recite the blessing and sound the horn over them, and shalt rejoice over your Land on this day. It shall be the New Year of the Trees unto you; and thou shalt plant on every hill and mountain and in every glen and valley.'

"The children responded as one, 'We are here, ready to plant.'

" 'Strength and courage to you,' the leaders called out.

HAMISHAH ASAR BISHEVAT

"As the blue and white flag was unfurled to the breeze, the thousands of children and adults arose and joined the planters in the anthem TEHEZAKNAH. This was followed by a spring dance, beautifully executed by a group of girls, and by a new planting song, sung responsively by the chorus and the audience.

"Then the planters, in groups of three, carrying spades, hoes, and watering cans, marched to the platform to receive the saplings, singing as they marched. From hand to hand the plants passed, until every group had one. With the band playing and the chorus chanting, they walked in procession round and round the platform, in a new version of the traditional HAKAFOT ceremony on SUCCOT, and then struck out, twenty-four abreast, across the field towards Bialik Boulevard for the actual planting.

"On the wide boulevard, which a year ago was nothing but sand, the spot for each tree had been previously marked off by the city gardener. Every group of three children soon found a spot, and the work began. Those who carried the spades set to digging; those who carried the watering-cans hurried off to fetch water; while those who carried the plants waited patiently for the great MITZVAH, or privilege, of placing the roots into the soil. They worked fast, and soon every sapling was in its place, resting firmly in the compact earth, and drinking of the water so generously poured by the children.

"The band followed the planters and stationed itself in their midst. At a signal, the musicians began playing ET LATAAT, Time for Planting. In a second, spades, hoes, and cans were put away. The children joined hands, each group around its newly-planted sapling, and danced merrily, enthusiastically. They continued to dance until the band

113

changed to HATIKVAH. Planter and audience stood at attention as they sang the national anthem. And with this, the ceremony came to a fitting conclusion."

Palestine Day

In America and other countries, HAMISHAH ASAR is celebrated as Palestine Day. In schools, the festival is observed with special assemblies, classroom parties, and entertainments for parents. The plays, movies, recitations, songs and games all deal with Palestine, its geography and its products. The refreshments are fruits which grow in Palestine and sweets made in Palestine. Similar celebrations are held in community centers and synagogues. Often clubs and schools dramatize the Palestinian planting ceremony. Zionist organizations arrange mass-meetings, lectures, and conferences in honor of the holiday. In the United States, a national convention is held in Washington, D. C., to inaugurate the United Palestine Appeal.

At home, HAMISHAH ASAR is celebrated as in former generations. Palestine fruit is eaten, stories about the land and its products are told, and Palestine songs are sung.

Jews outside Palestine, too, have found a way of combining festivity with practical help to Palestine on HAMISHAH ASAR. Children buy Jewish National Fund tree certificates* in honor of parents, and parents as educational gifts to their children. The certificate is usually presented in a little ceremony which consists of appropriate songs and explanations. Classes and clubs also buy tree certificates for presentation to teachers, leaders, and members on HAMISHAH ASAR. The money is used for planting trees in Palestine.

* A tree certificate costs $1.50, which covers the price of the sapling and its planting.

Hamishah Asar Bishevat

The story of HAMISHAH ASAR is in a sense the story of Israel's love for Palestine and the dream of tilling its fields and tending its orchards once again. On HAMISHAH ASAR, Jews imagined themselves in Zion, walking over its hills and meadows, resting beneath the shady trees, and refreshing themselves with its luscious fruits. Now that Palestine is being rebuilt, HAMISHAH ASAR has become a day of planting, of spreading knowledge about Jewish achievement in Palestine, and of raising funds to replant the mountains, plains, and valleys of Eretz Yisrael.

Chapter 8

JOLLY PURIM

PURIM is the jolliest of all holidays. Only SIMHAT TORAH compares with it in joy and fun. On SIMHAT TORAH Jews show how happy they are to have the Torah; on PURIM they make merry to express their confidence that they will outlive every HAMAN.

The Story

The story of PURIM, so interestingly told in the Book of Esther, is well known. There we read that Ahasuerus was king of Persia and Media, reigning over one hundred and twenty-seven provinces. On one occasion he gave a magnificent banquet to all the notables of his country. During the feast he invited the queen, Vashti, to come and show her rare beauty to his guests. Vashti refused and was banished from the court. A Jewish girl, Esther, was chosen from amongst the most beautiful maidens in the land to succeed her.

Soon after Ahasuerus appointed one named Haman to the highest office in the country. The new premier expected all the people to bow down before him. When Mordecai refused to do so, Haman was greatly incensed; and upon learning that Mordecai was a Jew, he obtained the king's consent to have all the Jews in the empire wiped out. He cast lots* to choose the day, drawing the thirteenth of ADAR.

When Mordecai heard of this, he notified Esther at once, urging her to speak to Ahasuerus on behalf of her people. The queen hesitated at first, for the king was not aware of her Jewish origin. In the meantime, Mordecai saved the life of the king by reporting a plot against him. As a reward Ahasuerus ordered Haman to parade Mordecai through the streets.

Esther finally gathered courage to speak to the king. When Ahasuerus learned the truth, he ordered Haman to be hanged and appointed Mordecai chief vizier. He also issued a proclamation permitting the Jews to defend themselves on the fatal day. When the thirteenth of ADAR arrived, the Jews were prepared, and they defended themselves so well that they were able to celebrate the following day. The struggle in Shushan, the capital, continued for two days, so that there they could not begin festivities until the fifteenth of the month.

* The name of the holiday, Purim, means casting of lots.

JOLLY PURIM

Mordecai's Letter

"Mordecai wrote these events down," the Book of Esther tells us, "and sent letters to all the Jews that were in all the provinces of the king Ahasuerus, both high and low, to enjoin them to keep the fourteenth day of the month ADAR, and the fifteenth day of the same, yearly . . . and they should make them days of feasting and gladness, and of sending portions to one another and gifts to the poor. And the Jews took upon them to do as they had begun and as Mordecai had written to them."* Ever since then Jews all over the world have celebrated PURIM each year. The rabbis of the Talmud are quoted as saying that PURIM will not be eliminated even when Messiah comes.

Although Mordecai's letter mentioned two days of holiday, only one day has been observed, in recent generations on the fourteenth day of ADAR, by all Jewish communities. On the preceding day, pious Jews fast in honor of Esther, who abstained from food for three days before approaching the king with her plea. Persian Jews keep this fast as strictly as the Day of Atonement. The day following PURIM is known as SHUSHAN PURIM, memorializing the Jews of Shushan who had to continue their self-defense for two days and could not celebrate until the fifteenth of ADAR. On a leap year, PURIM is observed in the second ADAR.

Questions and Explanations

Just when in Jewish history the PURIM episode happened no one knows. The Book of Esther mentions no dates and nowhere else is the story retold. Scholars believe that the event took place soon after the completion of the Second Temple. Equally puzzling are some of the facts in the story.

* Ch. IX, 20-23.

119

The Jews of Persia were only a handful among countless millions. How could they have defended themselves so successfully? The explanation seems to be that the story of PURIM occurred in only one part of the country, where the Jews were numerous and strong. By the time the narrative was written down, several generations later, it became magnified, as often happens to stories when they are passed on orally for many years.

Purim Literature

Only a few scholars have concerned themselves with the date and accuracy of the story. Among the people it was not questioned. In fact, as centuries passed, numerous tales and legends in connection with PURIM were created, found today in a special MIDRASH, popularly known as TARGUM SHENI. One of the tales would have it that Haman had been Mordecai's slave and barber at one time, which explains his actions against Mordecai and the Jews when the slave rose to power. Another legend describes how the trees refused their lumber for the gallows Haman planned for Mordecai. It remained for the thorn bush to come to Haman's aid, for, the bush said, "As I am the thorn so likewise is Haman a thorn that would scratch and tear Thy harmless people."

So lively a holiday would naturally give rise also to poems, plays, and humorous stories. Gifted poets like Eliezer Kalir, Abraham ibn Ezra, Solomon ibn Gabirol, and Judah Halevi composed special poems and songs for the occasion. In modern times, famous writers like Shalom Aleichem, Peretz, and Mendele Mocher Sefarim have written charming PURIM stories. Also plays for presentation on PURIM are regularly composed. Today we have a large number of PURIM plays, stories, poems, songs, legends, and anecdotes.

JOLLY PURIM

Other Purims

Several Jewish communities are known to have celebrated more than one PURIM each year in memory of days when they were saved from other Hamans.

The Jews of Egypt observed CAIRO PURIM for many years to celebrate the day of miraculous delivery on ADAR 27, 1524. The leader and protector of Egyptian Jewry was then Abraham de Castro, who held the high office of Master of the Mint for the government. One day the governor of the country suggested that all new coins be struck with his name on them instead of that of Selim I, the Turkish sultan who also ruled over Egypt. This would have meant treason and de Castro refused. But when a written order arrived from the governor, de Castro fled to Constantinople where the sultan lived. The Jews of Cairo were left to the mercy of the governor, who proceeded to threaten them with plunder, imprisonment, and death if they did not raise a large sum of money by a certain date. Fortunately, his treachery was discovered in time and he was beheaded.

Another PURIM, known as VINCENZ PURIM, occurred a century later in Germany. Then, as now, the Jews were blamed for the hard times in the country. Vincenz Fettmilch, a baker, declared himself a "new Haman" and organized an attack on the Jews. The ghetto of Worms was first to suffer. Frankfort was next. Fortunately, the elector or governor Frederic considered these pogroms acts of civil disobedience. He gathered a strong force of cavalry, infantry, and artillery and quickly put down the riots. The "new Haman" was hanged and the other rioters were compelled to pay damages to the Jews. The Jews of Frankfort instituted a special PURIM on ELUL 27, 1614.

Jewish Holidays and Festivals

Purim in the Synagogue

PURIM is celebrated in the synagogue, in the home, and in the community. Among western Jews the home and synagogue observances have been most festive, while among Sephardim and other Oriental Jews the community celebrations have been more colorful. In Persia, a PURIM service and celebration is held at Hamdan, where the traditional tombs of Mordecai and Esther are said to be found.

The Evening Service

When a person says that he is going to the synagogue on PURIM he means one thing—to hear the MEGILLAH—for that is the distinctive PURIM custom observed in the house of worship. The MEGILLAH, a scroll which contains the story of Esther as told in the Bible, is read in the evening and the following morning, by the HAZAN or by a learned person whom the congregation wishes to honor. Oriental Jews usually accord this honor to a bridegroom.

Gifts to the Poor

Mordecai's injunction to give gifts to the poor on PURIM is carried out in the synagogue in a traditional manner. Each person, even the poorest, drops a coin, usually a half dollar, into the plate as he enters. The half-dollar is in remembrance of the half-shekel which Jews contributed in Adar toward Temple repairs and sacrifices. In some communities, this money was given to individuals who planned to settle in the Holy Land. Today a special plate is provided for contributions to the Jewish National Fund for buying land in Palestine.

As part of the service, a special PURIM prayer is said, offering thanks for the wondrous triumph over Haman. After SHAHARIT, at the morning service, the Sefer Torah is taken out and a brief selection is read,* describing the battle between the Israelites and the Amalekites in the desert, for according to tradition Haman was a descendant of Amalek.

Reading the Megillah

Reading of the MEGILLAH on PURIM has been for many centuries a most enjoyable custom. During the first two chapters, the synagogue is comparatively quiet. The noise begins with the opening sentence in the third chapter where the full name of Haman appears. Thereafter, every time Haman is mentioned the noise-makers start anew. Strictly speaking, only the full name, giving his ancestry and his origin, should receive such treatment, but the boys refuse to be concerned about such details.

Haman receives particularly rough treatment in oriental synagogues. Boys come armed with pop-guns and toy pistols. The men and women depend on their feet for stamping and their fists for hammering at the arch-enemy. But not all. Some write the hated word on a stone and strike on it zealously. The more nimble scribble it on the soles of their shoes and then proceed to stamp Haman out of existence. Among Ashkenazim or western Jews, the GRAGER or rattler is the favorite noise-maker.

CELEBRATION IN THE HOME

If for some good reason members of a pious family are unable to go to synagogue on PURIM, the MEGILLAH is

* Exodus XVII, 8-16.

brought home and read there. The home, however, has two PURIM customs of its own, which are as old as the festival itself: the SEUDAH and SHALACHMANOT.

Shalachmanot

SHALACHMANOT is one of the reasons why young and old in every generation have looked forward to PURIM. Among Sephardic Jews it is as important as Christmas gifts among Christians. Parents give gifts to children. Relatives and friends exchange presents. Gifts are made to rabbis and teachers. Engaged couples would feel offended if they did not receive a valuable present from one another. The poor and needy, of course, are not forgotten. Non-Jewish friends and employees, too, are on the list.

Cakes, candy, and fruit have been, as they are today, the popular SHALACHMANOT items, although books, wearing apparel, and other useful articles are sometimes sent. Sephardic children like best cakes baked in various shapes—MEGILLAHS, Queen Esther, Mordecai riding on a horse, Elijah blowing the SHOFAR, Messiah mounted on a donkey, and the like. The Jewish confectioners in Jerusalem and other oriental communities vie with one another in baking the most interesting PURIM figurettes.

SHALACHMANOT to the poor has been donated in various ways. At one time, money would be collected to provide poor brides with dowries, and to ransom Jewish captives. Beggars were given coins and food. The half-shekel collected in the synagogue was sent to the Rabbi Meir Baal Ha-Nes fund in Palestine. Some of these customs still exist in East European and oriental Jewish communities. In America PURIM baskets are often presented to poor families, and contributions are made to various Jewish funds.

JOLLY PURIM

Purim Seudah

In many homes the PURIM gifts are given out to members of the family at the SEUDAH or feast on PURIM night. Only the SEDER on PESACH and the first meal in the SUCCAH compare with the PURIM SEUDAH as a happy family dinner. Unlike the other two, however, the SEUDAH has no ceremonial.

Food and drink are of the best. In addition to bread, HAMANTASCHEN are eaten. In the soup, KREPLACH are universally preferred. For the main dish, turkey is popular, since Ahasuerus reigned from India unto Ethiopia, and the Hebrew name for turkey is cock of India. Another favorite dish are BUBB or BUBBELACH, large beans boiled in salt water. They are eaten, so we have it, in memory of Daniel's diet of cereals. Cookies in special PURIM shapes complete the traditional menu.

HAMANTASCHEN, known as far back as Abraham ibn Ezra's time in Spain, eight hundred years ago, are the favorite PURIM delicacy. The HAMANTASCH is three-cornered because Haman's hat was shaped that way. The mixture of crushed poppy seed and honey captured the palate of Jews to such an extent that they compared it to the biblical manna.

Purim Spielers

But food and drink, without PURIM entertainment, do not make the feast a PURIM SEUDAH. In former generations, this was provided by PURIM SPIELERS or actors who made the rounds from house to house. The characters in the plays were the well-known PURIM heroes: Ahasuerus, who resembled the local sheriff; Haman, modeled after the town drunkard; Vashti, who looked like a fat wash woman; Esther, a shy young maiden; and Mordecai, a fellow with a long beard and a big hunch on his back.

125

Though PURIM SPIELERS are rare today, the SEUDAH custom is widely observed. Everywhere PURIM night is celebrated around the family table with good food and drink, with song and story and general merriment. Clubs and organizations also arrange banquets and parties.

Purim in the Community

PURIM has been the great community festival of the year—the day of carnivals, masquerades, bonfires, banquets and minstrel plays. All these forms of PURIM fun may best be seen in Palestine. But in other countries also, including America, PURIM is celebrated in schools and community centers, by clubs and organizations, and even in the streets. Most picturesque of all is the PURIM ADLOYADA in Tel Aviv.

Purim Plays

Plays and minstrel shows were presented in schools and public auditoriums as well as in homes. The largest crowds flocked to the YESHIVAH, curious to see how the serious students of the Talmud caper and frolic once a year. The master of ceremonies, one of the boys, was called the "PURIM rabbi." Today PURIM plays are as popular as ever, and are presented by schools, clubs, and community centers. In Tel Aviv the story of PURIM is enacted annually on a huge outdoor stage before an audience of ten thousand or more.

Carnivals and Masquerades

For the carnival idea on PURIM we evidently must thank the Jews of France who introduced it many centuries ago.

126

JOLLY PURIM

From France the idea spread to other countries. In America the indoor carnival has become popular in recent years, thanks to the famous ADLOYADA of Tel Aviv. Let us pay an imaginary visit to an old-time carnival and, after that, to the grand affair in Tel Aviv.

On PURIM morning the whole community gathers in the town square immediately after the MEGILLAH reading. The square is alive with masqueraders in every variety of dress. The orchestra is there, too, tuning up while the paraders form their lines. At last everything is ready. The band strikes up and the carnival is on. First comes Noah with his family. After him trail the animals—tigers, bears, wolves, lions—roaring, skipping, dancing. Joshua is next, followed by seven priests blowing trumpets, and by his warriors armed with kitchen utensils. After them come David and Goliath, Solomon with his wives, Jonah and the whale, and others from "Who's Who" in the Bible. Down the main street they go, stopping at the homes of prominent citizens. At each stop the antics, songs, parodies, and dialogues prepared for the occasion are repeated. The streets ring with laughter and song all day until late into the night.

Adloyada in Tel Aviv

Tel Aviv, the all-Jewish city, is "a gathering of exiles" from every country of the world. On PURIM one may see in Tel Aviv every kind of PURIM festivity. But being a modern city, it has fashioned out of the old customs a new festival and has given it a Hebrew name—ADLOYADA.*

---

* Literally the word means "until one does not know." The Talmud says that on Purim one should be merry to the point where he does not know whether Mordecai is to be blessed and Haman cursed, or the other way around.

JEWISH HOLIDAYS AND FESTIVALS

Clubs, schools, business associations, theaters, and homes begin preparations for PURIM several weeks ahead. By PURIM evening the city is not to be recognized. The streets, shop windows, public buildings, and even private homes are decorated with PURIM designs and symbols. On public squares and main intersections, huge colorful arches await the parade on the morrow.

The festivities begin the day before and continue far into the day following Purim. The theaters show special Purim plays. For the children there are merry-go-rounds, rides on camels, puppet shows, and masquerade parties. Young people and adults go to dances, maskballs, and theaters. In the evening and morning of Purim day, the synagogues are crowded with children and adults who come to hear the MEGILLAH. The stores sell HAMANTASCHEN and other Purim sweets, while the postmen are loaded with SHALACHMANOT parcels.

The big Purim event is the parade of floats and masks. There are serious floats, depicting the growth of the Jewish settlement, the increase in farms and factories, and similar achievements. Many of the masks are humorous, showing the lighter side of life in Palestine. Some are historical, enacting scenes from the Bible and from the history of Zionism. Individuals and groups of masqueraders march along, singing, dancing, and performing stunts. The biblical characters are all there, including Noah with his roaring animals. The Yemenites usually enact the story of Esther as part of the parade.

A quarter of a million people line the streets to witness the colorful march. Sidewalks, roofs, and balconies are crowded with spectators, among them many Arabs who come to see the Jewish "fantasia" as they call it.

128

JOLLY PURIM

PURIM IN AMERICA

In America, too, Purim is widely celebrated. Were we to visit a number of homes, synagogues, schools, and community centers on Purim we should find practically all the important customs being observed.

In the home, SCHALACHMANOT and the SEUDAH are the two chief customs. Relatives and friends exchange gifts in person, by messenger, or by mail. The poor are remembered, of course. Many homes make special contributions to charitable causes, while others present Purim baskets to poor families. Purim night finds relatives and friends gathered around festive tables for a SEUDAH. Old and new Purim songs are sung, Purim stories are read, and questions relating to the holiday are discussed.

As a community festival, Purim is celebrated in America with plays, entertainments, and masquerades. Purim carnivals, held indoors, have become popular in recent years, due to the Tel Aviv ADLOYADA. These carnivals usually consist of humorous Purim games, floats depicting scenes from the book of Esther, booths for selling refreshments and Palestinian products, a postoffice for exchange of messages and gifts, a procession of costumes and masks, and similar features. The income from admission tickets and sale of goods is donated to some worthy Jewish cause.

The custom of reading the MEGILLAH brings together large numbers of men, women, and children in American synagogues. Children come prepared with gragers and other noise-makers. The rabbi usually delivers a brief sermon, explaining the significance of Purim to past generations as well as to ourselves. As elsewhere in Jewish communities, all who come on Purim are expected to make contributions to charity and to the Jewish National Fund.

Purim each year bids the Jew have courage and hope. There have been Hamans before; the Jews have suffered terribly, but they have survived them all. We shall survive the Hamans of this generation as well. We must not, however, depend on miracles, but must fight the evil on many fronts — by working for peace and democracy in the world; by rebuilding Palestine; by helping the victims of persecution to find new homes; by improving and strengthening Jewish life in every home and in every community; and by performing our duties as citizens loyally and intelligently.

Chapter 9

PESACH THEN AND NOW

PESACH, the favorite holiday of the Jewish people, has been observed continuously for over three thousand years. Beginning as a simple shepherd feast, it later became a national holiday, marking the birth of the Jewish nation. At the same time it developed into an agricultural festival.

Above all, Pesach has been the great festival of freedom, commemorating the emancipation from slavery and the exodus from Egypt. By this Passover ideal, Jews have meant freedom for every person to live in accordance with his faith and ideals, freedom for the Jews to live as a nation in Palestine, and freedom for every people to live in its own country and under its own government.

EXODUS AND FREEDOM

The Exodus is considered the most important event in all Jewish history. For over two hundred years Jews had been slaves in Egypt. They settled in the Nile country, the Bible tells us, at the invitation of Joseph. When later the Pharaohs launched an ambitious building program, the Hebrews were forced into service and gradually became slaves. How intense was their suffering is vividly described in the Book of Exodus.

At last a leader arose — Moses — who brought them out of bondage. They were free to march to the land promised to their forefathers. The Exodus proved to be the birth of the Jewish nation. Their common suffering as slaves served to unite the tribes, and to give them the goal of living as a free people in a country of their own.

It was natural that this great event should be remembered ever after, and that the day of emancipation should become a national holiday for all times. Centuries later, the rabbis of the Talmud said, "In every generation, every Jew should see himself as if it were he who was redeemed from slavery in Egypt."

AGRICULTURAL FESTIVAL

The march from Egypt to Palestine proved to be long and eventful, and the conquest of the Promised Land equally difficult. But finally the goal was attained, and the Jews established themselves there as a nation.

PESACH THEN AND NOW

The Jews were now farmers, tilling the soil for a livelihood. The important occasions of the year were the har-
vests, and since Pesach marks the beginning of the grain
harvest, it came to be celebrated also as an agricultural festival. Every farmer brought an OMER or sheaf of newly-cut
barley as an offering of thanksgiving to God.

The Omer Ceremony

"Ye shall bring the sheaf of the first fruits of your harvest
unto the priest," the Bible prescribes. "And he shall wave
the sheaf before the Lord, to be accepted for you." We
can picture the farmer and his family happily cutting the
first ears of barley in the field, binding them carefully into
a sheaf, and then carrying the precious bundle to the hill-
top where the place of worship was usually situated. There
many farmers awaited their turn. They sang and chanted
together. At length each reached the priest and handed the
sheaf of barley to him. The priest took the bundle and
waved it this way and that, intoning an appropriate prayer.

The Paschal Lamb Feast

In order to remember Pesach as the festival of freedom,
the Hebrews observed the paschal lamb ceremony. This
feast reminded them of the sacrifice every family offered
on the night preceding the departure from Egypt. How this
rite was performed in ancient Palestine, may be seen today
by a visit to the Samaritans* on SEDER night, for they ob-

---

* The Samaritans are descendants of an ancient people whom the Assyri-
ans settled in Samaria, Palestine, after the northern kingdom of Israel was
destroyed by Sennacherib. They are now a small sect, numbering about
150, and observe strictly many of the ancient Mosaic rites and customs.

serve it very much as prescribed in the following quotation from Exodus:

> They shall take to them every man a lamb, a lamb for a household. . . . And the whole assembly of the congregation of Israel shall slaughter it at dusk. . . . And they shall eat the flesh in that night, roast with fire, and unleavened bread. . . .And thus shall ye eat it: with your loins girded, your shoes on your feet, and your staff in your hand; and ye shall eat it in haste.
>
> Exodus XII.

A Two-Fold Festival

Thus Pesach became a two-fold holiday — the feast of freedom and the Spring agricultural festival. Both meanings were symbolized by the paschal lamb, by the OMER ceremony, as well as by the MATZOT. MATZOT reminded them of the unleavened bread prepared in haste by the Hebrews when they left Egypt; it thus became a symbol of liberty. To us the MATZOT also recall the bread baked from the first grain harvested by the Jewish farmers in ancient Palestine, and suggest the agricultural significance of the festival. They called it PESACH or Passover because the angel of death had passed over the homes of the Hebrews during the night of the plague of the first-born in Egypt.*

* Some scholars believe that Passover was celebrated as far back as Abraham's time. Our ancestors then were nomads, tending to their flocks of sheep and goats, which were their chief source of livelihood. The most important time of the year for them was the lambing season in the spring. More lambs and kids meant more milk and cheese for food and more wool for tents and clothes. At the conclusion of this period they celebrated. Each family roasted a young animal and made a feast, to which guests were invited. It was a festival of thanksgiving. They probably called it Pesach because this Hebrew word also means skipping, and refers, so some think, to the gamboling or skipping of the lambs and kids in the new pasture.

134

The name Passover must have also reminded them of the passing over or crossing of the Red Sea.

In First Temple Days

After the Temple built by Solomon became the chief center of festival celebrations in Palestine, thousands of pilgrims from all parts of the country gathered in Jerusalem to take part in the sacrifices and ceremonies on Pesach, as well as on Shavuot and Succot. This made Pesach a truly national festival. In one of the books of the Bible, we read:

> And the king (Josiah) commanded all the people saying: 'Keep the passover unto the Lord your God, as it is written in the book of the covenant.' For there was not kept such a passover from the days of the judges that judged Israel, nor in all the days of the kings of Israel, nor of the kings of Judah; but in the eighteenth year of King Josiah was this passover kept to the Lord in Jerusalem.
>
> Kings II, xxIII, 21-23.

IN SECOND TEMPLE DAYS

Pesach gained in importance after the Babylonian exile. During the exile, the Jews learned to treasure freedom and independence more than ever before. Those driven to foreign countries realized what it meant to have a country of their own. Those who remained in Palestine tasted the bitterness of living under strange rulers. When the Jewish nation was finally reestablished and the Temple rebuilt, Pesach was observed with far greater devotion than in preceding generations.

By this time, most of the books of the Bible had already

been written down. Now the Jews could read the sad story of enslavement in Egypt and the accounts of the heroic Exodus. They could also study the commandments to observe the festival as well as laws regarding liberty and fair treatment of slaves and strangers.

Again and again in the Bible, the Jews are bidden to remember their emancipation from slavery and to celebrate the Passover. The main points specified are that the festival be celebrated seven days; that only unleavened bread or MATZOT be eaten; and that the first and last days be days of rest and festivity. The date prescribed is the fourteenth of Nissan.

Even more often does the Bible remind the people to live in accordance with the ideals of righteousness and justice. Remember, says the Bible repeatedly, that "thou wast a slave in Egypt." Therefore, treat your servants and other employees decently; respect your parents; be fair to strangers; do not mistreat even your dumb animals. No other experience in its long history has impressed itself so deeply in the hearts and minds of the Jewish people as their bondage in Egypt. It proved to be a lesson remembered in every generation.

Pilgrimage Festival

During the Second Hebrew Commonwealth, Pesach was celebrated both as a family feast and as a pilgrimage festival.

With the approach of the holiday the eyes of Jews from all parts of Palestine, as well as from neighboring countries, turned towards Jerusalem. From every town and village pilgrims set out for the capital city. Those who lived near took each a lamb with him. Those farther away purchased lambs in the sheep market at Jerusalem.

Pesach Then and Now

The ceremonies in the Temple must have been most impressive. Thousands of pilgrims and residents of Jerusalem awaited their turn to offer the paschal sacrifice in the Temple. They were admitted in groups of thirty. As each man slaughtered his lamb and the priests performed the various rites in silence and awe, the Levites accompanied the ceremony with the singing of the HALLEL and with instrumental music.

The Home Ceremony

From the Temple, the lamb was taken home and there roasted on an open fire. The home ceremony resembled our own SEDER in many respects. The youngest son asked the Four Questions, which were answered by reading portions from the Bible relating how the Jews were enslaved in Egypt and how they became a free people. MATZOT were eaten, the four cups drunk, bitter herbs dipped in vinegar, and similar customs observed. Long after the roast lamb was consumed and the feast completed, the family sat up, listening to stories and explanations of the holiday. The pilgrims performed the SEDER in the Temple court or in their tents on the outskirts of Jerusalem.

Pesach in the Middle Ages

When the Temple was destroyed by the Romans and the Jews ceased to live as a nation in Palestine, they continued to cling to the ideals for which Pesach stands and to observe the festival with great zeal. Both the national and the agricultural meanings of the holiday remained. Living dispersed in exile, they longed for liberty and independence. Exile was considered a kind of slavery. They prayed to be free to live as Jews without fear of persecution. Torn away from the soil, the people longed for Palestine and hoped to till its fields once again.

Inquisition Days

No threat of danger could prevent our forefathers from celebrating the festival. During the Inquisition in Spain, when Jews were forced to become Christians, they observed the SEDER in secret chambers and cellars at the very risk of life. Many a Jewish home was raided on Pesach night by the Inquisition spies, and many a Jew was dragged from the festive table direct to the dungeons, or to be burned alive at the stake.

Blood Accusations

During the Middle Ages, Jews were often accused of using the blood of Christians for the SEDER ceremony.* Hundreds and perhaps thousands of Jews during the past centuries paid with their lives because of this barbarous slander, and many Jewish communities were attacked and pillaged on Pesach. As late as 1910, a Russian Jew, Mendel Beilis, was tortured for years in prison because he was falsely accused of having killed a Christian child for Pesach purposes.

PASSOVER IN OUR OWN TIMES

And so Pesach has come down to our own times as the most important Jewish festival of all. The mode of observance has undergone change during the course of the cen-

---

* When Christians were still a minority, they too were subjected to this false accusation.

turies. More laws and customs were added, and a special prayerbook, the HAGGADAH, was composed. Pesach became essentially a home festival, with the SEDER the dramatic event of the whole holiday. But in the synagogue, too, it has been observed with special prayers and ceremonies. For a picture of devout observance, we must go back to the time of our grandfathers, or travel to a Jewish community in Poland, or to Palestine. Let us, therefore, describe some of the customs as they were observed by our grandfathers, and some as they are observed among ourselves — the preparations, the SEDER, the synagogue service, and other festivities.

Preparing for Pesach

Preparations for Pesach, in our grandfathers' generation, began immediately after Purim and continued until the afternoon of the first SEDER. For there was plenty to do — baking MATZOT, preparing new clothes, house cleaning, getting ready the Pesach dishes, learning the Haggadah, and more. The children, free from school beginning with the first of Nisan, had a large share in these preparations. On the Saturday preceding Pesach, known as SHABBAT HAGADOL or Great Sabbath, parts of the Haggadah were read in anticipation of the festival.

Baking Matzot

Baking MATZOT was the big task. There were no MATZAH factories in those days, so that the residents of every village and town had to provide the unleavened bread for themselves. The wafers were baked cooperatively, several families working together for at least a week or more. The largest house, with the best oven, was turned into a bakery.

139

Only special flour, harvested and milled under the watchful eye of a pious rabbi, was used. (Wheat flour and pure water are the only ingredients of MATZAH.)

House cleaning was the next task. This combined both spring and Pesach cleaning. The walls were whitewashed inside and out. All furniture received a vigorous scrubbing, and bed-clothes a thorough airing. On SEDER night the Jewish neighborhood looked bright and cheerful as at no other time of the year.

Maot Hittim

In the midst of all these preparations, Jews did not forget those too poor to provide themselves with MATZOT and other Pesach necessities. A special collection known as MAOT HITTIM or Coins for Wheat was made in every Jewish community in order to help the poor observe Pesach properly.

Getting Ready the Pesach Dishes

Helping mother with the Pesach dishes was great fun for the children. First of all, the Pesach plates and pots had to be taken down from the attic or up from the cellar, where they were kept all year. Immediately after, the HAMETZ dishes were put away. Only older boys and girls, of course, were permitted to handle the breakable articles. Then came the job of kashering the silverware and metal pots so that they could be used on Pesach. This was accomplished by washing and polishing them thoroughly and then dipping them in boiling water for a few minutes. In every neighborhood a large kettle of water was kept boiling all day

for that purpose. Young children were sometimes teased
by threats to kasher their mouths for Pesach with boiling
water.

Clearing out the Hametz

All this scrubbing and scouring was not considered suf-
ficient. A special ceremony known as BEDIKAT HAMETZ or
clearing out the leaven was performed the night before the
SEDER. Armed with a feather duster, a tallow candle, and a
wooden spoon, father and children proceeded from one
corner to another and from one window sill to the next to
gather up any crumbs left behind, as well as crumbs of
bread placed there by design. This was accompanied by a
special prayer which the father and children recited. Next
morning, the spoon, feather duster, and their contents were
burned on an open fire in the yard. This ceremony was
called BIUR HAMETZ.

No matter how thoroughly the house was cleaned, one
could not be sure that all HAMETZ had been cleared out.
And what of the HAMETZ dishes and provisions left over?
And grocery stores? They could not throw out all the
over-supply of HAMETZ foods. So anxious were the people
that Pesach be observed strictly, that all HAMETZ belongings were sold to a non-Jew for the duration of the week,
and a bill of sale was written out. This was usually done
by the rabbi of the community who would "sell" all the
HAMETZ property of his followers with the understanding
that the bill of sale was to be returned immediately after
the holiday.

One who has not taken part in all these preparations can
hardly imagine how much work was involved, and how
gladly and cheerfully it was done. Uncle Pesach, as one

folk song refers to the festival, comes only once a year, and what a welcome guest he is! On SEDER night, every Jew felt more than rewarded for all his labor and expense.

The Haggadah

So anxious have Jews been to celebrate the SEDER properly that a special book known as the Haggadah or *the story* was compiled for the occasion. Many centuries passed before the present Haggadah was completed. Some of its contents, like the HALLEL prayer, were recited in the ancient Temple by the Levites during the paschal lamb sacrifice, while some of the biblical selections which tell about the enslavement and emancipation, were read in the homes. Several chapters of the Haggadah were later added from the Mishnah and Talmud. Many of the songs and chants are of more recent origin. The famous Had Gadya ballad, for example, is only several hundred years old. Today, there are many attractive editions of the Haggadah, illustrated with beautiful designs and pictures.

THE SEDER CEREMONY

At no other time of the year is the home as festive as on SEDER night. Children who have been at a real SEDER remember it all their lives, and they long for the occasion no matter where destiny may take them in later years. The SEDER has everything — ceremony, songs and stories, games and pranks, good food and drink. There are serious moments and moments of merriment. It is a pageant with every one taking part, re-enacting the ancient story of liberation, reminding the Jew of his eventful history, and rekindling hope for the future. It unites families and friends.

Jews who are persecuted feel free on that night. Children may ask all the questions they wish.

Arranging the Seder Plate

Before beginning the ceremony, the father prepares the SEDER plate, which in some homes consists of beautifully inlaid metal. He takes three MATZOT, places one over the other, and covers them with an embroidered Pesach napkin. The MATZOT stand for unity. The top one represents KOHEN or priest; the middle one is called LEVI or Levite; the third is known as YISRAEL or Israelite. All Jews, father explains, whether KOHANIM, Levites or Israelites, are brothers. Today we have other divisions among our people: orthodox, Reform, conservative, radical; Zionists and non-Zionists; Ashkenazim and Sephardim. All, however, celebrate Pesach; and Pesach, in turn, helps to bind them to one another and to keep alive the ideals of freedom and righteousness.

In the right-hand upper corner of the plate, father puts a shankbone to represent the paschal lamb. In the opposite left-hand corner, he places a roasted egg, for the Hagigah * sacrifice offered in Temple days. In the center of the plate, he lays down the MAROR or horseradish, to recall the bitterness of slavery. In the lower right-hand he puts a heap of HAROSET, a concoction of nuts, apple, and wine which looks like the clay and bricks which our ancestors made for Pharaoh. In the left-hand lower corner, he places a sprig of parsley, a symbol of spring, of life and hope. Father arranges the objects until he is satified that they are attractively laid out.

* The festive offering of the pilgrims to the Temple on the Three Festivals.

The Seder Begins

After all preparations are completed, the family is seated at the table. Besides the parents and children, there are several relatives and friends. The father reclines on pillows to symbolize the spirit of freedom and comfort which Jews feel on this night of nights. The table is tastefully set, with the candlesticks, flowers, and wine glasses adding beauty and cheer.

The ceremony follows a set procedure. The very meaning of the Hebrew word SEDER is order or procedure. There are three parts: the Haggadah, the meal, and the prayers and songs after the meal. Father depends on the younger children to keep track of the ceremonial order.

Kiddush and Other Customs

First is KADESH — chanting the KIDDUSH prayer by the head of the family, and also by the other men and older boys. The KIDDUSH expresses thanksgiving for the holidays and for the joy and cheer they bring. The wine glasses have been filled beforehand. Usually each member of the family has his own favorite wine glass. Elijah's cup is also poured.

After all wash their hands, comes the ceremony of KARPAS. Each person dips a leaf or two of parsley into salt water, makes the proper benediction,* and eats it. The parsley is a symbol of spring and growth; the salt water represents the tears shed by enslaved and oppressed Jews.

Now the children begin watching father's every move, as he breaks the middle MATZAH and puts away the larger

* "Who createth the fruit of the earth."

144

half between the pillows. They are planning how this precious AFIKOMAN may be taken away. For the one who succeeds is entitled to a reward in the form of a handsome gift.

Maggid — Chanting the Haggadah

The Haggadahs are opened and the chanting begins. Those who know Hebrew join in. Some parts are also read in English in many homes. The first selection is a hymn of welcome: All who are hungry come and feast; all who have no SEDER of their own come and join. It also expresses hope for the future, when all men will be free and the Homeland in Palestine be rebuilt.

The Four Questions

Now comes the turn of the youngest child to ask the famous Four Questions: Why MATZOT? Why MAROR? Why dip twice? Why recline on pillows? The selections that follow are in answer to these questions. The family reads in unison paragraph after paragraph, story after story. Usually questions are asked about events connected with the Exodus. Sometimes a discussion arises. The parents explain the more difficult passages for the sake of the younger children.

The Four Sons

One selection in the Haggadah describes four different kinds of sons — the wise, the wicked, the simpleton, and "the son who does not know how to ask," and tells what remarks each makes about the SEDER. Father explains that this may also refer to four kinds of Jews: the loyal devoted Jew, the indifferent or disinterested, the ignorant, and the one who does not even know that he is a Jew.

The Four Cups

Altogether four cups of wine are prescribed for the SEDER. Why four no one knows surely. Some think because in ancient times the number four had some special meaning. Others say because of the four promises made to our ancestors when they were freed from Egypt: "And I will take you out" of the land of bondage; "And I will save" you; "And I will free" you from slavery; "And I will take" you to be a chosen people.

The chanting continues, recounting the suffering in Egypt, the plagues sent upon Pharaoh, the escape from bondage, and the crossing of the Red Sea. There are explanations of why MATZOT and the bitter vegetables are eaten. There are also prayers of thanksgiving. Some of the selections are sung in unison.

The Seder Meal

After an hour or more of story and song, which is concluded with the drinking of the second cup of wine, the meal is served. It begins ceremoniously. First hands are washed. Then two benedictions are recited over the MATZOT, as each one helps himself to a piece. This is followed by the MAROR. The horseradish is dipped into HAROSET and the appropriate BERACHAH recited before it is eaten. Then a sandwich of MATZAH and the ground MAROR is eaten. This, the Haggadah tells, is in accordance with a custom of the sage Hillel.

The meal itself, as becomes a festive occasion of this sort, is of the very best the family can afford. In some homes roast lamb takes the place of chicken, for obvious reasons. The two special dishes are egg soup and KNAIDLACH. The egg soup is a concoction of hard boiled eggs and salt water.

PESACH THEN AND NOW

The knaidlach are matzah balls. Vegetables other than parsley and horse-radish are not eaten in many homes, so that
those two symbols of the festival may not lose any of their
importance. The special plates, glasses, and silverware add
a great deal to enjoyment of the meal.

Finding the Afikoman
For dessert, the afikoman is eaten. This serves to remind
us that in olden times each person received a small portion
of the pascal lamb for dessert. After the Temple was destroyed, the afikoman consisted of sweet ingredients. Still
later it was changed to a piece of MATZAH. There is much
merriment at this point of the SEDER, for the prescribed
dessert has disappeared. Father turns to the children, who
blame one another. Finally, the guilty one confesses and
agrees to return the precious piece — at a price. Father, of
course, will not hear of it, and even threatens to continue
without the afikoman. But he gives in at last, promising a
gift to the lucky one. Every person then receives his crumb
for dessert. The meal is concluded with the chanting of
grace.

Once more the Pesach books are opened. By this time the
younger children are tucked away in bed, even those who
insisted that they would sit up to see the prophet Elijah
come in and sip from his wine-cup. Children who are
neither too young nor too old are given nuts to play with,
in order to keep them awake. This may be the origin of
nut games on Pesach. The older folks proceed with the
songs and prayers in the second part of the Haggadah.

Elijah's Cup
Now comes the ceremony of opening the door. Some

147

declare that this is done to admit the prophet Elijah, who is said to visit every Jewish home on SEDER night. Elijah, according to legend, will announce the coming of the Messiah, who is to lead the return of the Jews to Palestine. On SEDER night, perhaps more than at any other time, Jews have prayed and hoped for redemption from exile and for the rebuilding of Palestine. Others believe that opening the door expresses the spirit of freedom and safety which Jews feel on this occasion, in spite of the blood-libel and other false accusations.

Formally, the SEDER ends with "Next Year in Jerusalem!" repeated three times. Actually, the family refuses to leave the table, for the most lively melodies are still to be sung — ADDIR-HU, the charming EHAD MI YODEA, and the tuneful HAD GADYA. For good measure, in many homes modern Hebrew and Palestinian songs are sung late into the night.

Seder Variations

In some distant communities we find slight differences in the SEDER ceremony. Bucharan Jews, for example, begin with a sort of play. No sooner is the family seated than a guest comes in. He carries a pack on his back and a staff in his hand. His clothes are tattered, like one who has traveled a long distance. He is welcomed, invited to sit down, and then the SEDER begins.

Caucasian Jews do not have a SEDER plate. Instead, the Pesach symbols are embroidered on a large table cloth. They, too, commence the feast with a playlet of welcome. One of the guests leaves the room. After a few minutes, he knocks on the door, begging to be admitted. "Who are you?" he is asked. He answers, "I am a descendant of Abraham, Isaac, and Jacob, and come all the way from ypt to celebrate the festival with my brother Jews." He is finally admitted, and the reading of the Haggadah begins with joy and enthusiasm.

Community Festivities

Most Jews celebrate two SEDARIM, for the same reason that other holidays are observed two days. Reform Jews keep only one SEDER. In Palestine also, only one is celebrated.

In recent years a new custom has become popular — a third SEDER. This is in accordance with ancient tradition in Palestine when Pesach was observed both as a community and as a family festival, the community celebration taking place in the Temple at Jerusalem. Today Jews gather for a third SEDER in a synagogue or center. In addition to the dinner and the Haggadah, a special program is presented, consisting of musical and dramatic numbers as well as a talk on the significance of Passover in our own times. In many conservative synagogues, the second SEDER is observed as a community affair, while some Reform temples arrange a community SEDER on the first night. Most Jews, however, prefer to celebrate the festival at home and have the children enjoy the beautiful ceremony in the proper and traditional manner.

Pesach festivities continue for eight days. The first two and the last two days are devoted to synagogue services and family parties, while on the middle or HOL HAMOED days men perform their regular daily labors. Above all, Pesach is the time for visiting relatives and friends. The special cakes and sweetmeats make these visits particularly enjoyable. Nut games are the favorite pastime of both children and adults during Pesach week. Schools, centers and synagogues present concerts and plays.

Jewish Holidays and Festivals

In the Synagogue

A festive spirit prevails in the synagogue during the week of Pesach. There are holiday prayers and appropriate readings from the Torah and Prophets. On the morning of the first day, the TAL or Dew prayer is chanted, asking for abundant dew in Palestine during the summer months when no rain falls in that country. Even though far away, Jews have recited this prayer throughout the centuries to express their attachment to the Homeland and their hope of its rebuilding. On the second night the counting of the OMER begins. (See Lag Beomer for an explanation of this custom.) The other Pesach prayers recall the story of the Exodus and the ceremonies in the Jerusalem Temple. The HALLEL is recited daily. Readings from the Torah * tell of the Exodus and of the Temple ceremonies on Pesach.** It is also customary to read the Song of Songs, perhaps because there we find a beautiful description of spring in Palestine.

Pesach in Modern Palestine

Pesach is the great family festival in Palestine. For days ahead, trains and buses are crowded with passengers traveling to spend the holiday with relatives and friends. City people go to the colonies, while country folk stream to the cities. Many observe the ancient custom of pilgrimage by celebrating Pesach in Jerusalem.

Every Jewish home in Palestine is lavishly decorated with flowers. Perhaps the passage from the Song of Songs, which

---

* Especially Exodus XII, 21-51; XIII, 17; XV, 26; Numbers XXVIII, 16-25.
** The chapters from the Prophets speak of peace and freedom in the future for Israel and all mankind. Ezekiel XXXVII, 1-14; Isaiah X, 32; XII, 6.

describes the spring season in Palestine, has inspired this new custom:

> For, lo, the winter is past,
> The rain is over and gone;
> The flowers appear on the earth;
> The time of singing is come,
> And the voice of the turtle is heard in our land;
> The fig tree putteth forth her green figs,
> And the vines in blossom give forth their fragrance.
>
> Song of Songs, II, 11-14.

Stories of a New Exodus

At the SEDER, the Haggadah is supplemented with stories, poems, and songs of the new redemption. One tells how he escaped a life worse than slavery in Germany. Another relates his wanderings over snow-capped mountains or sun-parched deserts or stormy seas to freedom in the Homeland. A third recalls the "bread of affliction" he and his fellow HALUTZIM lived on for several years until the neglected soil of Palestine began to yield abundantly. They tell and sing of the new exodus of Jews from lands of persecution, and of the hardships they bravely bore to lay the foundations of the Jewish National Home. After the SEDER, they dance the horah and the other new Palestinian dances.

Omer Ceremony Revived

In some of the colonies the ancient OMER custom has been revived, for now, as then, Pesach marks the beginning of the grain harvest in Palestine. The dining hall is decorated with appropriate pictures and slogans, and with flowers and ears of grain. The ceremony begins when the children, dressed in the garb of ancient Jewish farmers and carrying

151

sheaves of newly-cut barley, enter the room singing. They march up to the platform and lay the sheaves before the head of the village, who receives the offering with appropriate words. The whole gathering then chants songs of thanksgiving for the fruits of their labor, vowing to continue their work until all of Palestine becomes fertile once again, and the Jewish Homeland is finally rebuilt.

On Pesach Jews remember the story of liberation from slavery. They also recall how, in spite of wandering and persecution for so many centuries, the Jews have survived and preserved their faith and culture. In their darkest days, Pesach gave Jews hope that they would be saved, even as their ancestors in Egypt were redeemed from slavery, and that freedom and peace would be enjoyed by all peoples. American Jews compare Pesach with Independence Day, for both holidays stand for freedom and democracy. Coming as it does in the springtime of the year, Pesach seemed to say to the Jew in every age: As spring follows winter, so are brighter days sure to come after trouble and suffering.

Chapter 10

LAG BEOMER

LAG BEOMER, the youngest of all Jewish festivals, recalls the last attempt of our ancestors to regain independence as a nation in Palestine. On Lag Beomer we remember the bravery of Bar Cochba and his followers who fought to reestablish the Jewish nation, and the equal bravery of Akiba, Bar Yohai, and other scholars who upheld the right of the Jews to live in accordance with the Torah.

THE BAR COCHBA REVOLT

It happened about sixty years after the Temple in Jerusalem had been burned down by the Romans, or eighteen

155

centuries ago. Palestine lay in ruins. Jerusalem was razed to the ground and the same lot had befallen hundreds of towns and villages. Tens of thousands had lost their lives in the long wars with the Romans. Countless thousands were exiled or sold into slavery. Many escaped to neighboring countries.

Our ancestors, however, did not give up hope. They began to rebuild the ruins at once. Farmers went back to their fields and orchards, and artisans to their work-benches. The scholars of the time established schools to carry on Jewish learning and the observance of Jewish law. One of them acted as NASI or head of the people. Synagogues took the place of the Temple in Jerusalem, and prayer was substituted for sacrifice. They expected that before long Jerusalem would rise again, and the holy Temple be rebuilt.

Grievous was their disappointment when they learned that Jerusalem was to be rebuilt as a Roman city, and that on the site of the Temple a place of worship to the Greek god Jupiter would be erected. Seeing their hopes shattered, the Jews revolted, for they wished to free themselves from Roman rule and to reestablish their own nation in Palestine. Leaders of the revolt were Bar Cochba and Akiba, one an able general, the other a great scholar. Some looked to Bar Cochba as the long-awaited Messiah.

Victorious at First

They were successful at first. The Romans were driven out of a large part of the country, and Judea was declared an independent nation. New coins with Bar Cochba's name were put into circulation as a sign of independence. A large army sent by Rome to suppress the revolt was defeated by Bar Cochba and his followers.

LAG BEOMER

Rome, however, was too mighty. Soon an even larger army overran Palestine, reconquering region after region and city after city. Bar Cochba entrenched himself in the city of Bethar, where he held out for many months. But finally the Roman battering rams broke down the walls of the last stronghold. The fall of Bethar and the death of Bar Cochba put an end to the last attempt of the Jews to rebuild their nation in Palestine. Not until modern times have the Jews made any serious effort to recreate their Homeland.

Another Kind of Heroism

The Romans followed up their victory on the battlefield with cruel persecutions intended to wipe out the Jewish religion and culture. Laws were decreed forbidding circumcision, observance of the Sabbath, and teaching of the Torah. Anyone disobeying these laws was severely punished or put to death. The great Akiba and nine other foremost scholars of the day were tortured until they died. No amount of persecution and torture, however, could force the Jews to give up their religion and Torah. They continued to live in accordance with Jewish law despite every peril.

WHY LAG BEOMER

Out of this heroic period in Jewish history has come to us the festival of Lag Beomer. The name itself tells us only the calender-date of the festival. LAG stands for the Hebrew letters LAMED and GIMEL, which have a numerical value of thirty-three. OMER is the Hebrew word for a sheaf or measure of grain. In ancient times, when the Jews were an

157

agricultural people, they celebrated the beginning of the harvest by bringing an OMER of barley on the second day of Pesach as an offering of thanksgiving. They counted seven weeks from that day, celebrating Shavuot on the fiftieth day. These forty-nine days came to be known as OMER or SEPHIRAH days, SEPHIRAH meaning counting. Lag Beomer is observed on the thirty-third day from the second day of Pesach, or the eighteenth day of the Hebrew month IYAR.

Scholars' Day

During the Bar Cochba revolt, tradition tells us, a terrible epidemic struck the students of Akiba in the Omer season. No less than twenty-four thousand young men lost their lives. On Lag Beomer the epidemic suddenly stopped. Akiba and his students were so highly regarded by the people that the Omer weeks were declared a period of semi-mourning, when no weddings and other celebrations were allowed. Only on Lag Beomer proper was festivity permitted, and it came to be known as Scholars' Day.

Simeon Bar Yohai

Another tradition links this day with the great teacher Simeon Bar Yohai, who lived at the same time. Because he had refused to obey the Roman decree against the study of Torah, and continued to teach his pupils, his life was steadily in danger. He succeeded in escaping to a cave in the mountains of Galilee. For thirteen years he lived with his son in this hideout, feeding on the fruit of the carob tree and drinking from a nearby spring.

Each year, his students paid him a visit on Lag Beomer. Lest the Roman soldiers suspect their destination, Bar Yohai's students disguised themselves as hunters and car-

Lag Beomer

ried bows and arrows. The story further has it that Bar Yohai died on Lag Beomer. His last request to his disciples was that the day of his death be observed by celebration rather than by mourning. To this day, his burial place at Meron is the scene of a very joyous Lag Beomer celebration.

Two other events are said to have happened on that day. The manna eaten by the Israelites in the desert on their long journey from Egypt to Palestine, came down for the first time on the eighteenth of IYAR, which is the date of Lag Beomer. The second event was the beginning of Haman's downfall, when he led Mordecai through the streets of Shushan.

Lag Beomer Customs

The story of Lag Beomer lives on in its customs. Nowhere in the ancient books do we find an account of the holiday. Even the prayerbook does not contain any special selections or blessings for the occasion. Only by knowing the customs and their explanations are we able to piece together the story of the festival.

A Day of Weddings

The period between Pesach and Shavuot, known as SEPHIRAH, is considered a time of mourning, in honor of the thousands of Akiba's pupils who were killed by an epidemic. Hair may not be cut, no dances or concerts may be held, and no weddings are permitted, among other restrictions. Lag Beomer, the day when the plague is said to have stopped, has become, therefore, a day of happy events, particularly of weddings. With so many festal oc-

159

currences, Lag Beomer is truly a happy festival in thousands of Jewish communities throughout the world.

A Day for Outings

To children Lag Beomer has been a day for outings and picnics. Even the pupils in the old-fashioned HEDER permitted themselves this luxury. Armed with bows and arrows, they proceeded with their teacher to the woods to spend the day there. The weapons were reminiscent of Bar Yohai's students who disguised themselves as hunters when they went to visit their beloved teacher at Meron. Or perhaps they served to remind them of Bar Cochba's brave attempt to win independence.

The picnic lunch consisted of hard boiled eggs, bread and butter, cookies, and fruit. Each boy brought as much as he could, the rich bringing more and the poor less. The teacher would collect all the lunches and then divide the food equally among the pupils. After this cooperative luncheon, the children had contests and played games with the bows and arrows. Having had enough of play, they sat down under a shady tree and listened, enraptured, to the Lag Beomer stories as related by their teacher.

Jewish schools and clubs in all parts of the world are today carrying on this Lag Beomer custom. Hebrew schools usually arrange their annual outing on or around Lag Beomer. Bow and arrow contests and other games, pageants and playlets depicting Lag Beomer events, as well as appropriate songs and stories, constitute the program of the day.

A Persian Jewish Custom

Among Persian Jews, Lag Beomer is a day of thanksgiving feasts. When illness or misfortune befalls a Persian

Jew, he turns to the Zohar for courage and guidance, and vows to arrange a thanksgiving feast on Lag Beomer in honor of Bar Yohai, who is believed to be the author of this great book. Such vows are made during the year by many families. On Lag Beomer, therefore, practically everyone attends a feast either as host or as guest. The homes are decorated with beautiful Persian rugs; food and wine are served generously; while entertainment is provided by musicians who sing and play appropriate songs. As part of the celebration, the final chapter of the Zohar is read and explained to the guests.

Festival at Meron

Nowhere in the world is Lag Beomer celebrated with so much joy as at Meron, a village near Safed in Palestine, which is said to be Bar Yohai's burial place. Hundreds of pious Hasidim from all parts of Palestine and from neighboring countries come to Meron to honor the great teacher and the ideals for which he stood. While waiting for the celebration, they chant psalms, sing hasidic songs, and study the Zohar, the holy book ascribed to Bar Yohai.

The real festivities begin when a huge bonfire is lit at midnight. The women throw silken scarfs and other valuable clothing into the flames. The men, young and old, sing and dance around the fire until early morning. Many, however, fall asleep from sheer exhaustion. Soon, every one awakened with the call "SHAHAR BA," the dawn has come. An unforgettable sight greets their eyes as the hues of the crimson dawn light up the mountains and valleys all around. Praying and chanting begin anew. Then the three-year-old boys receive their first haircuts, and the hair is thrown into the flames, accompanied by ecstatic singing and dancing.

This celebration draws to Meron hundreds of modern Palestinians, as well as tourists, many of whom take part in the festivities.

Lag Beomer Campfires

As a result of the Meron celebration, the bonfire idea has spread to all parts of Palestine. In Jerusalem, Tel Aviv, and Haifa, as well as in the colonies, children and youths light huge campfires on Lag Beomer evening. Thousands gather around to sing and dance and to hear the ancient stories about Bar Cochba, Akiba, and Bar Yohai. In other countries, too, Jewish schools and clubs are beginning to celebrate in this manner. When the weather or distance does not permit outdoor celebrations, indoor campfire programs are arranged in America and other diaspora lands.

LAG BEOMER IN AMERICA

In common with Jews the world over, many American Jews observe practically all the Lag Beomer customs here described. Weddings, outings, campfire programs, and similar festivities may be witnessed in every community where Jews are found.

In quite a number of cities, Lag Beomer is observed as Jewish Book Day, and the week during which it occurs, as Jewish Book Week. This is a most fitting manner to celebrate the festival, for Lag Beomer is also Scholars' Day, recalling the learned Rabbi Akiba and Rabbi Simeon Bar Yohai, as well as their associates and disciples. Accordingly, exhibits of Jewish books are arranged in Jewish institutions and also in public libraries. Lists of new and old Jewish books are distributed, and lectures on Jewish literature held. These activities are intended to acquaint young and old with the Jewish literary treasures and to encourage the reading of Jewish books.

When Lag Beomer falls on a Sunday, another new custom is noticeable everywhere — young men and women selling flowers on behalf of the Jewish National Fund. The moneys collected are used to purchase land in Palestine for Jewish settlement. Lag Beomer has thus also become Flower Day. If the festival falls on a week-day, Flower Day is postponed to the following Sunday.

The festival of Lag Beomer recalls a heroic chapter in the long and eventful history of the Jewish people. It no longer merely commemorates, however, the last serious attempt to reestablish the Jewish nation in Palestine. For today, the ancient country is becoming the Jewish homeland once again. The story of Lag Beomer inspires Jews to work for Palestine, as well as to devote themselves to Jewish learning and religious ideals. Moreover, the customs of the holiday, especially the outings, campfires, and celebrations, add joy and beauty to our life as Jews.

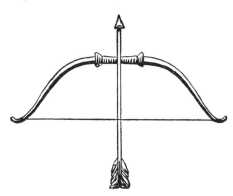

Chapter 11

SHAVUOT FESTIVAL

THE SYMBOLS of Shavuot are honey and milk, flowers, green branches, and, of course, the two tablets of the Law. The honey and milk stand for Torah and learning. The Torah, our sages said, is sweet as honey and nourishing as milk to those who study it and who live in accordance with its teachings. The flowers and green branches stand for land and crops, symbolizing the farm life of our people in ancient times and in our own day. The tablets recall the great event on Mt. Sinai. Shavuot is both a Torah festival and an agricultural holiday.

FEAST OF WEEKS

It is called Shavuot because this Hebrew word means weeks. In the early days, when Jews had no written calendar, the exact date of Shavuot was figured by counting seven weeks from the second day of Pesach, the holiday taking place on the fiftieth day. When a fixed calendar was later adopted, the sixth of SIVAN was designated as the date, which falls each year exactly forty-nine days after the second day of Pesach. But Shavuot or Feast of Weeks has remained the popular name of the festival to this day.

These seven weeks came to be known as the Omer season because they began with the Omer sacrifice* on the second day of Pesach. They are also called Sephirah days, SEPHIRAH being the Hebrew word for counting.** The great Maimonides said that Jews awaited Shavuot so anxiously that they counted every day from Pesach on, as one reckons the days before a most important personal event, like a Bar Mitzvah or a wedding.

Agricultural Festival

When the Jews lived as a nation in Palestine, Shavuot was primarily an agricultural festival. Most of our ancestors

---

* A barley sacrifice, marking the beginning of the harvest season.
** See Lag Beomer for a full explanation of Omer.

then were farmers. Shavuot marked the end of the grain harvest, for the sub-tropical climate of Palestine ripens the grain crops in the Spring. When the wheat and barley were safely stored away, the people gave thanks and rejoiced. They called the celebration HAG HAKATZIR, Festival of the Grain Harvest. In the fall they celebrated a second harvest festival, Succot, which comes at the end of the fruit season.

Shavuot day was observed in ancient times with home feasts and Temple ceremonies. It was the custom that no cereal offering of the new crop be made before Shavuot. When Shavuot arrived, every housewife ground fresh flour from the new grain and baked bread and cakes for the family feast. In the Temple at Jerusalem a special cereal sacrifice of two loaves baked from the new crop was offered. The sacrifices were accompanied by appropriate ceremonies, singing of hymns, and playing on harps and other musical instruments. Pilgrims in the thousands from all parts of the country took part in these Temple ceremonies.

Festival of New Fruits

The pilgrims did not come empty-handed. Each man brought the first of his barley, wheat, grapes, figs, pomegranates, olive-oil, and honey, the seven varieties for which Palestine was then famed. For Shavuot was also the Festival of First Fruits or HAG HABIKKURIM. We find a short but vivid description of this aspect of Shavuot in the Mishnah.

"How are the BIKKURIM selected?" the Mishnah asks. It answers: "When a man comes down to his field and sees a ripe fig, or a ripe cluster of grapes, or a ripe pomegranate, he ties each with a red thread, saying, 'These are BIKKURIM.'"

167

The description of the pilgrimage, freely translated, is as follows:

> "All the pilgrims from a section of the country gather in the chief city of the region, spending the night in the open. Next morning they are awakened early with the call: 'Awake, let us ascend to Zion, to the house of the Lord our God!'
>
> "Those living near Jerusalem bring fresh figs and grapes, while those from distant parts bring raisins and other dried fruit (carrying them in gaily decorated baskets). At the head of the procession walks the ox, his horns trimmed with gold and olive branches. They march on, accompanied all the way to Jerusalem by the playing of the flute.
>
> "At the gates, they are met by the elders as well as the artisans of Jerusalem, who greet them by saying, 'Enter in peace, our brothers from (mentioning the region).'
>
> "With the flute playing in front, they proceed to the Temple mount. There they are joined by the king, who also carries a basket on his shoulder and enters the forecourt of the Temple with them. In the forecourt, they are welcomed by the Levites with a hymn.
>
> "Holding the basket on his shoulder, each pilgrim recites, 'This day have I proclaimed unto the Lord.' Then the basket is lowered and handed to a priest, who waves it to and fro as he completes the chanting of the hymn. Finally, the basket is placed alongside the altar and the pilgrims leave the sanctuary."

Jerusalem was so crowded on Shavout that many pilgrims had to camp outside the city walls. But they did not mind. It was well worth the discomfort to see the capital city and to take part in the ceremonies. They had something beautiful to remember all their lives. They also felt happy to share their crops with others and to be able to offer thanksgiving to God for a plentiful harvest.

TORAH FESTIVAL

A time came when Shavuot took on an additional meaning. Mighty Rome appeared on the world stage, conquering nation after nation. Palestine met the sad fate of other countries. The Temple was burned, countless thousands were killed, and larger numbers were exiled or sold into slavery. The Jews were no longer a self-governing nation in their own country.

The Jewish leaders and teachers of the time proved far-sighted. Even before the sad end came, men like Yohanan ben Zaccai put their faith in Torah and learning as the means of saving the Jewish people. If only Jews hold fast to their Torah and religion, they declared, the Jewish people will live on. The great Akiba taught that just as fish cannot live out of water so the Jewish people cannot survive without Torah. Another rabbi is quoted as saying that Shavuot is the wedding anniversary of the Jewish people, and the Torah is the marriage certificate between the Jews and God.

Other teachers and scholars of those days described the importance of Torah or Jewish learning in various ways, but they all had the same idea in mind.

> *The more Torah the more life; the more schooling the more wisdom.*
> *It (the Torah) is a tree of life . . . and happy are those who guide themselves by it.*
> *Fix a definite time for the study of Torah.*

Do not say "I will study when I have leisure"; perhaps you will have no leisure.

Study of Torah which is not accompanied by good deeds must fail in the end.

Where there is no Torah there are no manners; where there are no manners there is no Torah.

He who honors the Torah will himself be honored by men.

Thus, at about this time in Jewish history, some twenty centuries ago, the other meaning of Shavuot gradually came to the fore. For it was at this season of the year, according to tradition, that the Ten Commandments were given to the children of Israel at Mount Sinai. A truly stupendous event was this in the life of the Jewish people, as the Bible account makes altogether clear.

The Great Event

"And it came to pass on the third day, when it was morning, that there were thunders and lightnings and a thick cloud upon the mount, and the voice of a horn exceeding loud; and all the people that were in the camp trembled. And Moses brought forth the people out of the camp to meet God; and they stood at the nether part of the mount. . . . . And the Lord came down upon Mount Sinai, to the top of the mount; and Moses went up. . . . And God spoke all these words (the Ten Commandments)."

Exodus xix.

What the Ten Commandments have meant to the Jewish people and to the rest of the world ever since that day is known to every one. They have proved to be not only

170

the foundation of Judaism but also the foundation upon which all modern civilization is based. When Jews say Torah they usually mean the Five Books of Moses, but Torah also stands for all the great Jewish teachings, for all Jewish learning.

Shavuot, then, became chief of the two Torah festivals, the other being Simhat Torah. On Shavuot Jews recall the great event on Mount Sinai. In Hebrew the festival is known as ZEMAN MATAN TORATENU, the Season of the Giving of our Law. More than this, on Shavuot Jews express their joy for all the great laws and ideals of Israel.

NEW SHAVUOT CUSTOMS

New ways of celebrating the holiday as a Torah festival developed. In the synagogue, the Ten Commandments and other appropriate selections from the Bible were introduced, as well as specific prayers. The most beautiful Shavuot prayer, AKDAMOT, composed by Meir ben Isaac Nehera in the eleventh century, tells of God's love, of Israel's devotion to Torah, and of hope for the Messiah when peace and goodness will reign in the world. An abridged Bible and Mishnah, known as the Tikkun, was composed, so that on Shavuot Jews might review the teachings of Judaism. Many stayed up all night to study the holy books. Even special dishes and delicacies were invented — honey cakes and cheese cakes, as reminders that the Torah is sweet and life-giving. The three days before Shavuot came to be known as SHELOSHET YEMEY HAGBALAH, for Moses, you remember, asked the people to prepare themselves within three days for the great event on Mount Sinai. These were devoted to the study of the Bible and other sacred books.

Synagogues and homes were decorated with green branches and flowers. This, too, was a reminder of the giving of the Ten Commandments on Mount Sinai which, legend has it, was unusually verdant on that memorable day. Some explain this custom by saying that on Shavuot the success or failure of the fruit harvest is determined in Heaven. It may be that the green branches were intended to remind the people that the Torah "is a tree of life." Children enjoyed the trip to the woods on the eve of Shavuot to pick flowers and branches and then help their parents decorate home and synagogue.

Dramatizing the Ancient Story

In some Jewish communities the scene at Mount Sinai was enacted on Shavuot. After the synagogue services, everyone proceeded to a hill on the outskirts of the town, where the transmission of the Ten Commandments was dramatized. Then followed a mock war between the forces of evil and the forces of good, which the "soldiers of good," of course, won. In this manner the importance of the festival, the duty to study and teach the Torah, and the hope for the days of the Messiah when all evil would be banished, were impressed upon the minds of the children. In other communities, short hikes to nearby fields and woods were the custom of the day, perhaps for the same reason.

A Boy's First School Day

It also became the custom to initiate young children into school on Shavuot, so that they might be introduced to study on this special day in honor of Jewish learning. Wrapped in a TALLIT, the boy was first carried to the synagogue by the rabbi of the community, accompanied by parents and friends. There the Ten Commandments were read to him from the Torah scroll — his first lesson. From the synagogue he was taken to the school or as it was usually called, the HEDER. Instead of a book, a slate was placed before him on which was written with honey the sentence, "Moses commanded us a Law, an inheritance for the assembly of Jacob." As he repeated each word, gifts of fruit and sweets dropped down on the table. He was told that these were thrown to him by angels from heaven to make his first day in school sweet and pleasant.

Harvest Festival Remains

With all these new customs, the old meaning of Shavuot as a harvest festival was not forgotten. Selections describing the ancient ceremonies were included in the prayerbook. The decorations of flowers and foliage were explained as representing the trees and flowers of Palestine. They also introduced the reading of the Book of Ruth, which beautifully describes the harvest in ancient Palestine, and recounts the charity customs in those days —how the poor were allowed to pick up the fallen ears of grain and the forgotten sheaves, and also to cut the grain left for them in the corners of the field. King David, too, was remembered, for according to tradition he was born at Shavuot time, and was a descendant of Ruth. To recall the BIKKURIM ceremony, Yemenite Jews served every kind of new fruit.

Shavuot Today

Thus Shavuot has come down to us as a two-fold holiday. In the prayers, ceremonies, and customs of today both the

Torah and the agricultural meaning of the festival are abundantly reflected.

At home, school, and synagogue, the old customs are observed by Jews the world over. Many homes and synagogues are decorated with flowers and green branches. Dairy dishes and delicacies are eaten, BLINTZES being particularly popular. The Book of Ruth is read, and also stories about King David. Learned Jews review the Tikkun on Shavuot night, while the very pious stay up all night studying the holy books. The appropriate prayers are read and chanted at home and synagogue. Schools present plays dramatizing Shavuot stories. Suitable home and club parties are held.

Confirmation

Reform and conservative congregations have introduced a new ceremony — confirmation. While in the Middle Ages children were initiated into school on this day, now it is the time for graduation exercises. Shavuot is an appropriate occasion for celebrating the completion of one period in a child's Jewish education, for Torah and Jewish education really are one. Some Hebrew Schools also hold their graduations at this season.

Bikkurim Ceremony in Palestine

In Palestine the old BIKKURIM ceremony has been revived. As in ancient times so today, the Jews of Palestine are engaged in gathering their grain at this time of the year, and at the end of the harvest they celebrate with appropriate ceremonies and programs. However, instead of all the festivities being centered in Jerusalem, as in olden days, celebrations are held in several places, while the BIK-

KURIM are given to the Keren Kayemet for the purchase of more land in Palestine.

The most colorful BIKKURIM celebrations may be seen in Haifa, where Jewish pioneers from the Sharon, the Emek, and the Jordan valley gather to offer their first fruits to the Keren Kayemet. The festivities begin with a procession and conclude with a pageant.

The streets of Hadar Hacarmel, the Jewish section of Haifa, are richly decorated for the occasion with flags, streamers, greenery, and electric lights. Most attractive are the arches of welcome at the entrance to Herzl Street, along which the procession passes. The sidewalks, porches, and roofs are crowded with thousands of spectators from every part of the country.

First in the procession are several thousand children, all dressed in white and wearing garlands of flowers and leaves. They pass in seven groups, representing the seven varieties for which Palestine was once famed.

Then come the youth from the colonies, carrying gaily decorated baskets filled with ripe fruits and vegetables, sheaves of freshly-cut barley and wheat, jugs of honey, young fowl, and bleating lambs. They are followed by trucks and wagons loaded with every kind of farm produce. The vehicles, too, are appropriately decorated. The "pilgrims" sing as they walk along, and their chants are echoed by the crowds on the sidewalks and verandas.

Cheerfully the procession winds its way to the amphitheater. After handing over the first fruits to the Keren Kayemet, the men, women, and children seat themselves in the open-air theater to enjoy the pageant, which is called HATENE or The Basket, re-enacting the ancient BIKKURIM ceremonies.

JEWISH HOLIDAYS AND FESTIVALS

In the first scene, on the huge stage, appear Hebrew pilgrims from Galilee, Gilead, Samaria, Judea, and other regions, all bound for Jerusalem. They exchange greetings and songs, and proceed together. The next scene is at the gates of the holy city, showing the reception of the pilgrims by the elders and working people of Jerusalem. The third scene is a dramatization of the ceremony in the Temple court where first fruits were received by the Levites and priests. The story of Ruth is also enacted scene by scene.

This old-new Shavuot custom has begun to spread outside of Palestine. In Poland, Lithuania, and other countries, including America, appropriate celebrations are held by school children and Zionist youth clubs. In Chicago, an impressive BIKKURIM festival is conducted annually in one of the city parks, and is witnessed by thousands of pupils and their parents and friends.

176

SHAVUOT FESTIVAL

Torah and Land

The meaning of Shavuot can be easily remembered by keeping in mind the names of the holiday. Shavuot stands for the seven weeks of harvest. HAG HAKATZIR, too, recalls the grain harvest in ancient Palestine and today. HAG HABIK-KURIM reminds us of the pilgrimage to Jerusalem and the first fruits ceremony. ZEMAN MATAN TORATENU stands for the giving of the Law and for the ideal of Jewish learning.

The customs of Shavuot are as revealing as the names. Reading the Ten Commandments, the Tikkun, and the Book of Ruth tells of both Torah and Land. Eating dairy dishes and honey cakes and decorating homes, synagogues, and centers with flowers and foliage are concrete symbols of learning and of soil. And the new ceremonies, confirmation in our own country and the BIKKURIM festival in Palestine, prove to us that the message of Shavuot is just as important in our own times as it has been in the past.

Chapter 12

TISHAH BEAV AND OTHER FAST DAYS

FASTING is an old custom among Jews, as it is among other peoples. Yom Kippur and Tishah Beav are the two important fast days, but there are a number of minor fasts kept by observant Jews throughout the world: Shivah Asar Betammuz, the Fast of Gedaliah, Asarah Betevet, and Taanit Esther.

On Yom Kippur Jews fast for religious reasons. Tishah Beav and the minor fasts are national memorial days — occasions to recall past calamities and to keep alive the hope and courage of the Jew. The American Memorial Day also serves this double purpose. When we pay tribute to the memory of the soldiers who lost their lives in American wars, we re-dedicate ourselves to the ideals of liberty, equality, and union for which they gave their lives. Likewise, on Tishah Beav and other Jewish fasts, Jews do not merely memorialize sad events, but also pray for the welfare of the Jewish people and for the rebuilding of the Homeland in Palestine.

WHY TISHAH BEAV

The Ninth of Av has been a day of tragedy in Jewish history. The greatest misfortunes in the long and eventful story of our people are said to have taken place on this day.

Tradition tells that the Israelites who had escaped Egyptian bondage were doomed to wander in the desert for forty years on Tishah Beav. Legend also has it that the spies sent by Moses to explore Canaan brought back their discouraging report on that day. "And all the congregation," we read in the Bible, "lifted up their voice and cried."

First Great Tragedy

However, the first real tragedy to take place on the Ninth of Av was the destruction of Solomon's Temple in Jerusalem by the Babylonians, in the year 586 B.C.E. With the burning down of the Temple, the First Hebrew Commonwealth came to an end. Thousands lost their lives; thousands were sold as slaves; and thousands upon thousands were exiled.

Second Temple Destroyed

Seventy years later, the new Temple was completed and the Jewish nation was reestablished on its own soil.

TISHAH BEAV AND OTHER FAST DAYS

And for about five hundred years the Jews lived as a nation in Palestine. Then came the next great national catastrophe. The Second Temple was destroyed, and again, according to the Mishnah, the misfortune was consummated on Tishah Beav. Great as the first blow was, this one far surpassed it in loss of life and property, and in its sad consequences for the future of the Jewish people.

Other Catastrophes

Sixty years later, the Jews made a final effort to regain their independence, under the leadership of Bar Cochba and Rabbi Akiba. For three years they waged a hopeless battle against mighty Rome. Bar Cochba and his brave followers made their last stand in the city of Bethar; and on Tishah Beav of the year 135 C.E. the Romans captured the city. A year later, once more on the Ninth of Av, Jerusalem was plowed under by the Romans and upon its ruins a Roman city was built. Ever since then the Jews have been dispersed throughout the world, without a country and government of their own. Only in recent times have they begun to rebuild the Homeland in Palestine.

How many more tragedies befell the Jewish people on this day of misfortune, no historian has as yet computed. Of one major event we do know — the expulsion of the Jews from Spain. It was on the Ninth of Av, in 1492, that at least 150,000 Jews were crowded into ships to seek new homes in new lands. In that same year, Columbus set sail on his great voyage of discovery.

In the twentieth century, two sad events took place on this day. On the Ninth of Av, 1914, Russia ordered mobilization of its army. This proved a decisive act in bringing

181

about the World War, which caused untold misery to the Jews as well as to other peoples. Fifteen years later in 1929, Arab riots broke out in Jerusalem on this day of misfortune.

SEASON OF NATIONAL MOURNING

Tishah Beav marks the conclusion of a period of national mourning which lasts for three weeks each year, the period beginning with the seventeenth of Tammuz. On that day, about two thousand years ago, the conquest of Jerusalem by the Romans had become so menacing that the offering of sacrifices had to be discontinued in the holy Temple. This day, too, known in Hebrew as Shivah Asar Betammuz, pious Jews observe with fasting and prayer.

The "Three Weeks"

Festivity and entertainment are forbidden during the "Three Weeks." No new clothes may be worn for the first time, no hair cut, no music played, and no weddings held. Only on the Sabbath, and on days of such special events as a Berit Milah or a Bar Mitzvah, is celebration permitted. Many Jews visit the cemetery during these weeks to pay their respects to dear ones who have passed away. On each of the three Sabbaths preceding the fast, certain chapters from the prophets foretelling tragedy and destruction are read in the synagogue. In the chapter from Isaiah, read on SHABBAT HAZON * before the fast day, the prophet says:

---

* It is called Shabbat Hazon because *Hazon* or vision is the first word of the chapter.

TISHAH BEAV AND OTHER FAST DAYS

Your country is desolate;
Your cities are burned with fire;
Your land, strangers devour it in your presence,
And it is desolate, as overthrown by floods.
And the daughter of Zion is left
As a booth in a vineyard,
As a lodge in a garden of cucumbers,
As a besieged city..........

Isaiah 1, 7-8

The "Nine Days"

As the three weeks advance and only nine days are left, the feeling of sadness increases, and more stringent rules are prescribed. No meat may be eaten, nor wine drunk, and no swimming is allowed. In school and synagogue the stories of destruction are read, and the warnings of the prophets are reviewed.

These customs serve as preparation for the great memorial day when Jews relive each year the tragedies which befell their ancestors. While on Pesach every Jew is called upon to imagine that it was he who was freed from Egyptian slavery, on Tishah Beav, in contrast, every Jew is expected to put himself in the place of his forefathers who with their own eyes saw the Temple in flames and Jerusalem in ruins.

It is in this spirit of reliving the past that Jews have observed Tishah Beav throughout the centuries. No flags are flown, no parades march, no bands are allowed to play. It is a day to be spent quietly in prayer, fasting, and lamentation. If the Ninth of Av falls on a Sabbath, it is postponed to the following day, since fasting is not permitted on SHABBAT, excepting Yom Kippur.

183

Tishah Beav Customs

The meal eaten before the fast includes eggs and a pinch of ashes. The eggs are eaten, according to one poet, because "eggs have no mouth and our grief is too strong for words." Ashes are used by Jews as a symbol of mourning on other occasions also. In the Middle Ages, the head of the family would deliver a short sermon at the conclusion of the meal on the importance of Tishah Beav. Today, the father usually tells his children some of the stories and legends about the destruction of Jerusalem.

In the Synagogue

On Tishah Beav evening Jews gather in synagogues. Before entering the house of worship it is customary to drop some coins for the poor, as well as for the purchase of land in Palestine, into special plates.

Now let us enter the synagogue. Very orthodox "shuls" are lit with candle light only. The people sit as mourners on the floor or on low benches. Their shoes are off. Their heads are bent over the Book of Lamentations. The cantor chants the poems and prayers in a melody that seems to come out of the very heart of the Jewish people.

Arise, cry out in the night,
At the beginning of the watches;
Pour out thy heart like water
Before the face of the Lord;
Lift up thy hands toward Him
For the life of thy young children,
That faint of hunger
At the head of every street.

Lamentations, ii, 19

TISHAH BEAV AND OTHER FAST DAYS

The following morning, lamentations are again chanted as part of the service, and also other appropriate hymns and prayers, which are included in the special prayerbook called KINNOT or dirges. These contain very vivid descriptions of some of the tragic scenes which took place when Jerusalem was conquered. The TALLIT and TEFILLIN are not worn during SHAHARIT, but instead at MINHAH in the afternoon.

After the morning service, it is customary to visit the cemetery. The day of national mourning becomes also a time for remembering relatives and friends no longer among the living.

Oriental Customs

In Palestine, visits are made on this day to the tombs of prophets and kings, and to the Wailing Wall. This is a particularly appropriate custom, since the wall is the only relic of the ancient Temple, which was destroyed on the Ninth of Av, in the year 70 C.E.

There are many quaint customs which are practiced only in certain Jewish communities. In East-European towns, boys play with burrs and with wooden guns, probably to recall the battles in ancient times. Another rare custom is sleeping on Tishah Beav with a stone for a pillow. Still a third is the practice among oriental Jewish women of anointing themselves with oil in the afternoon in honor of the Messiah, who is believed to have been born on this day.

Although Tishah Beav is no longer observed as strictly as in former generations, most of the customs described above are practiced by millions of Jews in European countries, in Palestine, in America, and throughout the diaspora. Reform Jews do not include Tishah Beav or any other fast

185

days, other than Yom Kippur, on the Jewish ceremonial calendar.

Sabbath of Consolation

The period of "**Three** Weeks," devoted to memorializing tragic events in Jewish history, concludes on a note of consolation and hope. For on the Saturday following Tishah Beav, known as SHABBAT NAHAMU or Sabbath of Comforting, the famous prophecy of hope from the book of Isaiah is read in the synagogue. This selection bids the Jew take comfort and be hopeful of the future.

> Comfort ye, comfort ye my people,
> Saith your God.
> Bid Jerusalem take heart,
> And proclaim unto her,
> That her time of service is accomplished
> That her guilt is paid off. . . .
>
> Isaiah XL, 1-2

THE MINOR FASTS

The seventeenth of Tamuz recalls two misfortunes. The first was the breach made in the walls of Jerusalem under the onslaught of the Babylonians, which was followed by the capture of the city and destruction of the Temple. The second event, some five hundred years later, was the stoppage of sacrifices in the Second Temple, due to the siege of Jerusalem by the Romans, which cut off all supplies from the holy sanctuary. No sacrifices have been offered by Jews as a way of worship ever since that day.

Another minor fast is ASARAH BETEVET or Tenth of Tevet. It, too, recalls an event which preceded the downfall of the First Hebrew Commonwealth. For on that day, some twenty-five centuries ago, Nebuchadnezzar the Babylonian laid siege to Jerusalem. Soon after, the city was taken and the Temple burned.

From that same period in Jewish history has come down to us a fourth memorial day — the Fast of Gedaliah, on the third of Tishri, the day after Rosh Hashanah. Gedaliah, a descendant of the royal house of David, was appointed governor of Palestine when the First Temple was destroyed by the Babylonians. With his appointment, hopes rose high among the Jews who remained in Palestine that this was not to be the end of their nation and independence. Unfortunately, Gedaliah was assassinated and their hopes vanished. So heartbroken were the Jews, that they proclaimed the day of his death * a fast. To recall the tragedy and to express their faith in the restoration of the Jewish people in Palestine, Jews have observed this fast ever since.

Finally, there is TAANIT ESTHER or the Fast of Esther, on the day preceding Purim. It is commemorated in honor of brave Esther, who fasted for three days before going to the king, Ahasuerus, to plead on behalf of her people.

Fasting and Hoping

The national fast days have been observed all these centuries because the Jewish people felt so keenly the loss of country and Temple. Each year they served as reminders of the time when Israel lived as a nation in Palestine, and strengthened their yearning for the homeland. The people also recalled the legend that Messiah was born on the very day when the Temple went up in flames. For Messiah, according to tradition, will lead the Jews back to Eretz

* According to tradition, Gedaliah was assassinated on Rosh Hashanah, but due to the holiday the fast was postponed to the following day.

Yisrael. This thought gave them courage to bear suffering. Even in the darkest days they hoped that some day, perhaps soon, Zion would be rebuilt and Israel restored in its own country. To this generation has been granted the privilege for which our ancestors prayed and fasted, for today the Jewish Homeland is being gradually rebuilt in the ancient land of Palestine.

Chapter 13

NEW ANNIVERSARY DAYS

PALESTINE has been the cradle of all but one * of our traditional holidays. The last festival to be born there was Lag Beomer. Now that the Jews are rebuilding the ancient land again, Eretz Yisrael is creating new holidays, or rather, anniversary days. In Palestine, as well as throughout the world, the following five days are widely observed each year:

* Purim.

189

Jewish Holidays and Festivals

Herzl Day — Tammuz 20
Balfour Declaration Day — November 2
Trumpeldor Day — Adar 11
Hebrew University Day — April 1
Bialik Day — Tammuz 21

Herzl Day

The first new anniversary to arise as a result of the rebuilding of Palestine was Herzl Day, in honor of the great Zionist leader Theodor Herzl. Each year on the twentieth day of the Hebrew month TAMMUZ,* Jews the world over pay tribute to his memory.

When Herzl was born in 1860, there was not a single Jewish colony in Palestine. The twenty thousand Jewish inhabitants lived in the four holy cities — Jerusalem, Tiberias, Hebron, and Safed — most of them dependent on charity for their existence. When he died at the age of forty-four, the first foundations of the Homeland were clearly visible, while throughout the world a large Zionist organization was in existence.

As a child, Herzl received the best education available in Budapest, Hungary, where he was born. He also had a Jewish teacher who taught him Hebrew, the Bible, and Jewish history. At the age of eighteen, Herzl entered a law school in Vienna, for his parents wanted him to become a judge. Six years later, he was graduated and was now called Dr. Theodor Herzl.

Herzl, however, wanted to be a writer, for which he showed talent very early. He soon gave up the law, there-

---

* This is the anniversary of his death. In Palestine, they are beginning to observe Herzl Day on the eleventh of Iyar, his birthday.

fore, and he devoted all his time to writing plays, articles, and stories. He made a living by contributing to newspapers. In his spare time, he wrote several plays which were presented in Viennese theaters. Soon Herzl won a name as a promising young author. During these years of study and composition, Herzl took no special interest in Jewish affairs.

The Dreyfus Trial

At the age of thirty-one, Herzl was sent to Paris as reporter for one of Vienna's most important newspapers. There in the year 1895, he witnessed the famous Dreyfus trial, which was destined to change his whole life.

Alfred Dreyfus, a Jewish captain in the French army, was falsely accused of turning over important government documents to the German government, of being a traitor to his country. It was clear to everyone that someone else had committed the crime and that Dreyfus had been made the scapegoat because he was a Jew. The protests from Emil Zola and other great men in France and other countries against this injustice, were in vain. Dreyfus was sentenced to exile on Devil's Island. Not until several years later did the Supreme Court of France recognize his innocence and free him from prison.

"The Jewish State"

Seeing how an innocent man was convicted merely because he was a Jew, Herzl began to ponder the sad lot of his people. Why must the Jews suffer so? How could this suffering be brought to an end? He sat days and nights at his desk thinking and writing, and the result was a book, "The Jewish State."

'The idea which I have developed in this pamphlet,"

Herzl wrote, "is a very old one. It is the restoration of the Jewish State. . . . The world resounds with outcries against Jews, and these outcries have awakened the slumbering idea. . . . It is now a question of showing that the dream can be converted into a living reality.

"We are a people — one people. . . . Yes, we are strong enough to form a State, and, indeed, a model State. We possess all human and material resources necessary for the purpose. . . . And what glory awaits those who fight unselfishly for the cause. . . . Therefore, I believe that a wondrous generation of Jews will spring into existence. The Maccabeans will rise again. . . . We shall live at last as free men on our own soil, and die peacefully in our own homes.

"If you will it, it is no dream."

Herzl's Achievements

When "The Jewish State" was issued, the first beginnings in Palestine had already been made. Jews from Russia and other countries had succeeded in establishing twenty-five agricultural colonies during the previous fifteen years. A wealthy French Jew, Baron Edmond de Rothschild, assisted the pioneers with land, loans, and instructors. Outside of Palestine, special clubs called HOVEVEY ZION or Lovers of Zion were organized to purchase land, recruit immigrants, and collect funds.

Herzl's book was hailed with joy by the HOVEVEY ZION as well as by other Jews everywhere, and they were most anxious to meet the author. When Herzl, as his first practical step, issued a call for a Zionist Congress, leaders from every important country responded promptly. For the first time in centuries Jewish representatives from all the world gathered voluntarily to plan the future of their people. They met Dr. Herzl and were inspired by his personality, sincerity, and ability. At this first Zionist Congress, held in Basle, Switzerland in 1897, a united organization was created and a definite plan of action adopted.

The purpose of Zionism, the Congress decided, was to create "a publicly recognized, legally secured home for the Jewish people in Palestine." This statement has come to be known as the Basle Program.

After this successful Congress, Herzl and his associates set out to win the consent of the nations of the world to the Zionist idea. What they wanted most of all was a charter from Turkey allowing the Jews to colonize Palestine, which was then part of the Turkish empire. They also sought the good-will of England, Russia, Germany, and other important countries.

While traveling about from one capital to another Dr. Herzl did not neglect the other practical work, building up a strong Zionist organization and colonizing more Jews in Palestine. Zionist Congresses were held regularly. A bank called the Colonial Trust Company was established to lend money on easy terms to settlers. The Jewish National Fund was founded to buy land in Palestine. The movement grew. Thousands joined the Zionist ranks, among them prominent men like Max Nordau and Israel Zangwill.

In the midst of all these activities, death came and took Herzl away. It was a fearful blow to Zionists and to all Israel. Herzl died because he had refused to spare himself. Repeatedly physicians had warned him that his weak heart could not long endure the strain of such continuous hard labor. But Zionism was too important an undertaking for Herzl to cease traveling about, organizing Zionist clubs, and writing books and articles. Herzl gave his life for his people.

It is to the memory of this great man, Herzl, that Jews pay tribute each year. He issued a call to organize for the rebuilding of Palestine, and the call was answered by the Jewish people. He interviewed kings and ministers and won the interest of the great nations of the world in the Zionist cause. He was the father of modern Zionism, and one of the great, inspiring Jewish personalities of all time.

On Herzl Day, Zionists arrange mass meetings to review the life of the great leader and to study his teachings. Jewish schools and youth clubs hold special assemblies and programs at which stories, plays, poems, and similar features describing the ideals and achievements of Herzl are presented.

BALFOUR DECLARATION DAY

Practical work to rebuild the Jewish Homeland in Palestine began over three score years ago. During the first decades, progress was rather slow, so that only about 100,000 Jews were settled in Palestine by 1914.

Palestine was part of the Turkish empire before the Great War. Theodor Herzl and the other Zionist leaders had tried steadily to obtain a charter to colonize Palestine. Turkey, however, not only refused to grant such a charter, but also placed many obstacles in the path of the pioneers. The other nations failed to understand the just claims of the Jewish people to their ancient land.

During the Great War, Palestine too became a battlefield, England having sent a large army to conquer the Holy Land from Turkey. As a result, much of what had been accomplished in Palestine with so much devoted labor was practically destroyed.

Negotiations with England

While the battle was raging in Eretz Yisrael, Zionist leaders were negotiating with the British government, proposing that the Jewish people be granted the long awaited opportunity to rebuild Palestine as their homeland. These negotiations proved successful. Great Britain had always been favorably inclined to the Zionist idea. Of all countries which Herzl and his associates had approached, England showed the most interest.

Great Britain, of course, was also looking after its own interests. It wanted to control Palestine because of the Suez Canal, which is to Britain what the Panama Canal is to the United States. The Suez Canal is a short cut for British ships carrying goods to and from India. By having Palestine developed as the Jewish National Home, Great Britain would have a friendly people in the country, and it would be more certain of free passage for British ships.

The Balfour Declaration

When victory in Palestine seemed certain, the British government made public its decision regarding the future of Palestine in a letter to Lord Rothschild. This letter has come to be known as the Balfour Declaration, because it was signed by Lord Arthur James Balfour, then Minister of Foreign Affairs in the British government. The Declaration reads as follows:

"His Majesty's Government view with favor the establishment in Palestine of a national home for the

Jewish people, and will use their best endeavors to
facilitate the achievement of this object, it being clearly understood that nothing shall be done which may
prejudice the civil and religious rights of existing non-
Jewish communities in Palestine or the rights and po-
litical status enjoyed by Jews in any other country."

The Balfour Declaration was received with great joy
by Jews the world over, for it recognized the right of the
Jewish people to their ancient homeland, and it promised
the Jews the opportunity to rebuild Palestine. Although
issued by Great Britain, it was first approved by France,
Italy, the United States, and many other nations. It was
the very charter which Herzl and his followers had unsuc-
cessfully tried to obtain.

Since the Balfour Declaration

Once before such a declaration had been given by a
great power to the Jewish people — the declaration proclaimed by Cyrus, King of Persia, some twenty-five hundred years ago. It permitted the Jewish exiles from Babylon
to return to Palestine and to reestablish the Jewish nation.
The Cyrus declaration proved successful; the Temple in
Jerusalem was rebuilt, the Jewish government renewed,
and the Jewish nation reconstituted. "May it be," Jews
prayed, "that the Balfour Declaration bring equally grati-
fying results."

Today we know that the Balfour Declaration has proved
to be a turning point in the history of Zionism. Palestinian
Jewry has grown to nearly half a million. Over two hundred
new colonies have sprung up, with factories, shops, schools,
synagogues, hospitals, and parks. The Hebrew language has

been revived and has become a spoken tongue once again. After centuries of neglect, Palestine has once more begun to bloom.

Each year, on November 2, Zionists the world over celebrate the great event.* In every Jewish community mass meetings, lectures, and entertainments are arranged. Palestinian movies, plays depicting the struggles of the HAL-UTZIM (pioneers), and the new Hebrew songs created in Palestine are usually part of the program.

TRUMPELDOR DAY

Trumpeldor Day was the third new anniversary to arise in the course of upbuilding the Jewish Homeland. It is observed annually on the eleventh of ADAR, the day when Joseph Trumpeldor and his brave comrades lost their lives while defending the colony Tel Hai in Galilee. This anniversary is also known as Hero Day, in honor of all the heroic pioneers who gave their lives for Palestine.

The rebuilding of Palestine has been a heroic task from the very beginning. The first pioneers who pitched their tents in the midst of swamps and sand dunes were indeed brave men and women. The SHOMERIM or watchmen who volunteered to stand guard over the Jewish colonies were even more courageous and self-sacrificing. During the Arab

---

* In 1939 Great Britain issued a White Paper which practically withdraws the promises contained in the Balfour Declaration. Instead of celebrating, Jews everywhere utilize this day to protest against England's breach of promise, and to increase work on behalf of Palestine. For the Jewish people are determined to continue rebuilding the Homeland, and are in hopes that Great Britain will yet live up to the Balfour Declaration.

197

riots of 1936-39, the heroism and self-restraint of the Palestinian Jews received the admiration of the whole world. Joseph Trumpeldor and his comrades have become the symbols of this heroism.

Trumpeldor was known in Palestine as the one-armed hero, having lost an arm while fighting in the Russian army during that country's war with Japan in 1904. He was not only decorated for his bravery but also had the distinction of being the only Jew promoted to the rank of officer in the czar's army. After the war, Trumpeldor, greatly shocked by the continuing mistreatment of Jews in Russia and in other countries, became a Zionist and left for Palestine.

For a number of year, Trumpeldor was happy, working as a farmer in the colonies. Then the World War broke out. Together with thousands of other Jews, he was obliged to leave the country, finding refuge in Egypt. While there, he organized the Zion Mule Corps as an auxiliary of the British army in the Gallipoli campaign. Soon this corps was disbanded and Trumpeldor went to England. Here a new task awaited him — organizing the Jewish Legion, which fought with the allied troops in Palestine until the country was conquered from Turkey.

Trumpeldor returned to Russia, but not to live there. His mission was to form an organization to recruit and train pioneers for Palestine. He even dreamt of organizing a Jewish army. He succeeded in establishing HEHALUTZ or The Pioneer, which has been in existence ever since and has prepared hundreds of thousands of Jewish youth for life and work in Eretz Yisrael.

Back in Palestine, Trumpeldor threw himself into the defense of the Jewish colonies against attacks by Arab bedouins. With true courage, he chose the most dangerous spot, the colony Tel Hai, in the north. And there, on the eleventh of Adar, 1920, he and six others lost their lives. But the colony was saved and is now one of the flourishing Jewish settlements in Palestine. Joseph Trumpeldor is remembered as a brave soldier, an industrious worker, and an inspiring leader.

HEBREW UNIVERSITY DAY

The idea of a Hebrew University in Palestine was conceived at the very time when the earliest pioneers were establishing the first colonies in the ancient land. Professor Herman Schapira, the man who first suggested the idea of the Jewish National Fund, was also first to propose the erection of a university in Jerusalem, as far back as 1882. He believed, and every one agreed with him, that the Homeland in Palestine should become the cultural center for all Israel. The building of schools and universities, therefore, must proceed hand in hand with the establishment of farms and factories.

After Professor Schapira died, Dr. Chaim Weizmann became champion of the idea of a Hebrew University. Several times it seemed as if a beginning would be made. But each time a new difficulty arose. Finally the foundation stone was laid by Dr. Weizmann in April, 1918.

Seven years elapsed between the laying of the cornerstone and the official opening of the university on April 1, 1925. Meanwhile several buildings were erected, a small park planted, an open-air amphitheatre constructed, famous scholars engaged as teachers, and students from many countries of the world enrolled. Dr. Judah L. Magnes of America was appointed head of the new institution of learning.

JEWISH HOLIDAYS AND FESTIVALS

The Opening Ceremony

Those present at the opening ceremony on Mount Scopus will remember that historic event all their lives. The newly-built amphitheatre was crowded with tens of thousands of Jews from Palestine and from all over the world. Some of the greatest universities in the world sent representatives. On the stage sat Lord Balfour, the Hebrew poet-laureate, Bialik, the great Jewish thinker, Ahad Ha'am, Sir Herbert Samuel, learned rabbis, Arab notables, Zionist leaders with Dr. Weizmann at their head, and many other prominent men and women. An artist was so inspired by the sight that he painted a beautiful mural of the scene. It is this festive opening of the Hebrew University which is celebrated by Jews the world over each year.

The University Today

It takes at least a half hour to walk through the campus of the University on Mt. Scopus, near Jerusalem. If we begin from the direction of Jerusalem, we see first the Medical School and Hadassah-Rothschild Hospital, only recently completed. Next we pass the Wattenberg Library, then the Students' House, and near by, the Institute of Jewish Studies. Farther up we see the Einstein Physics Building, the chemistry laboratories, the botanical gardens, the biological institute, the museum and the other buildings. Behind all these, to the East, is the amphitheatre. The land on which the school stands belongs to the Jewish National Fund.

These buildings indicate what is taught at the Hebrew University. Since it is a Jewish school, the Jewish subjects come first, Hebrew language, Hebrew literature, Bible, Talmud, Jewish history. Science is next in importance, including physics, chemistry, botany, and biology. Mathematics, too, occupies a prominent place. Among the foreign languages taught are Arabic, English, and French. Recently, courses in agriculture and medicine have been added. All subjects are taught in Hebrew.

The faculty of professors and instructors at the Hebrew University, which counted close to 150 men and women in 1940, includes many famous scholars, known all over the world for their books and discoveries. Quite a number are refugees from Germany and other fascist countries. The president of the Hebrew University is Dr. Chaim Weizmann, who is also a well-known scientist. The students, too, hail from many countries, the United States included. Over 800 young men and women were enrolled at the Hebrew University in 1940.

The University has been rendering valuable service to the welfare of Palestine. It trains Jewish scholars and teachers. Its archaeologists have been unearthing ancient synagogues and various antiquities. In its laboratories, scientists are discovering how to eradicate malaria and other diseases and how to improve the soil and crops of the country. The studies of the Arabic language and culture are helping to improve relations between Jews and Arabs. The books and magazines published spread knowledge and understanding in Palestine as well as throughout the world.

Friends of the Hebrew University

Because all Jews are interested in the University at Jerusalem, and because it is intended as a center of learning for Jewries everywhere, this school receives support from Jews the world over. The Board of Trustees of the University consists of Jewish scholars and leaders from many countries, including the United States. The Jews of America and England have been particularly helpful in building up the University. In America there exists an organization known as Friends of the Hebrew University, which collects funds for carrying on the work.

On April 1 each year, the Friends of the Hebrew University in every community gather to celebrate its official birthday. The programs consist of lectures and reports on the progress of the University and on the importance of Hebrew culture. Jewish schools, youth clubs, and Zionist organizations arrange special assemblies and meetings. Whenever possible, students who have been privileged to study at the Hebrew University are invited to speak.

BIALIK DAY

Bialik Day is the anniversary of the death of the great Hebrew poet, Hayyim Nahman Bialik, and is widely observed in Palestine as well as throughout the world, on the twenty-first of TAMMUZ. On this day, Jews pay tribute to the memory of Bialik and express their joy that Hebrew has become a living tongue once again.

When the Jews lived as a nation in Palestine, Hebrew was their national language. Young and old spoke Hebrew as their native tongue. Poets, priests, prophets, kings, and scholars conversed and wrote in Hebrew. The Bible, as you know, is an original Hebrew masterpiece. There were times when Aramaic and Greek were used in Palestine, but Hebrew remained the national language of the Jewish people.

When the Jews went into exile, they took the Hebrew language with them. However, it soon became the language of prayer and study, for in each country the Jews usually spoke the tongue of the people among whom they lived. Nevertheless, Jewish scholars, writers, and poets, with few exceptions, wrote in Hebrew at all times. It was also employed in contracts and other business transactions. Among the Sephardim, many could always speak Hebrew.

Hebrew and Palestine

During the many centuries of wandering, when the Jews prayed for a return to Palestine, they took it for granted that Hebrew would again be the spoken tongue in the Homeland. It was natural, therefore, that the rebuilding of Palestine should have been accompanied by the rebirth of Hebrew. Although there were Hebrew writers before the practical work in Palestine began, it was the return to Eretz Yisrael which made Hebrew a spoken tongue once again and which gave rise to a new Hebrew literature. Today, it is spoken in Palestine as well as by hundreds of thousands in other countries. Poets, novelists, scholars, and journalists are writing in Hebrew. Throughout the world, Jewish children and adults are studying the language, while in religious services Hebrew is used as in all preceding centuries.

The man who best symbolizes the rebirth of Hebrew is Hayyim Nahman Bialik. When he was born, in 1873, only one Jewish agricultural settlement had been established in Palestine. When he died, in 1934, there were close to 400,000 Jews there. At the time of his birth, Hebrew was largely the language of prayer and study. When Bialik died, Hebrew had become a modern, spoken tongue with a rich new literature. In this great change, Bialik played a most important role.

Bialik's Childhood

Bialik's childhood was spent in a Russian village. Little Nahman loved to play in the fields and woods near his home, to watch the sunsets, listen to the birds, pick flowers and berries in the summer, and make snowmen in the winter. He grew up with a deep love for nature, so much so that some of his best poems are about the beauties of nature.

He also loved books and knowledge. When his father died and Bialik, only seven years old, went to live with his grandfather, a new world was opened up to him — his grandfather's large library. There he spent many hours a day, devouring one book after another.

When he became Bar Mitzvah, he left the HEDER and went to the Bet Hamidrash, where he studied by himself, poring over the Talmud from early morning until late at night. So much did he love to study and read, that one of his finest poems is "Hamatmid," in which he describes and pays tribute to the devoted Jewish student.

Although studious and serious-minded, Bialik was a real boy, with a zest for play and pranks. His parents were very poor. Nahman knew early in life what it meant to be hungry. In his grandfather's home he did not lack bread, but he was unhappy because of the old man's severity. However, neither poverty nor severity could dampen his liveliness. This trait remained with him throughout life, so that as a man of sixty he was capable of frolicking with little children.

The poet in Bialik emerged at the early age of fourteen, when he began to write poems. At about the same time, he began thinking of the future, deciding to study for the rabbinate. Three years later, he packed up his few belongings and proceeded to the famous Yeshivah of Volozhin. There

Bialik continued to study the Talmud and other ancient books, and also to read modern works.

The Poet is Recognized

Young Bialik soon realized that his place was not at the Yeshivah but among writers. Only two years later, therefore, he left for Odessa, where Ahad Ha'am and some of the other new Hebrew writers lived. The young man had a hard struggle in the strange city, trying to earn a livelihood by tutoring. But he managed somehow. Far more important, he succeeded in making the acquaintance of Ahad Ha'am and the others, who at once recognized his abilities. When only nineteen, his first poem, "To a Bird," was published in a magazine, and was enthusiastically received everywhere.

From then on, Bialik lived and moved in the world of Hebrew literature. With every new poem, his popularity and fame grew. He wrote about the beauties of nature, about the Jew's love of learning, about poverty and persecution, about Palestine and the Jew's yearning for restoration, about love and hate, about mankind's dreams and hopes. He also composed lilting poems for children, for although childless himself he loved children dearly.

Bialik did not limit himself to poetry. He also wrote stories and essays, compiled the legends and sayings of the Talmud and Midrash, edited Hebrew magazines, translated great works from other languages, composed scholarly works, made an abridged version of the Bible for children, and engaged in other literary activities. Bialik was also a man of action. Together with two friends, he established and conducted a modern Hebrew school. Later he became head of a Hebrew publishing company. During the World

War, he worked tirelessly to protect and aid the war victims. At all times, he was active in Hebrew organizations and Zionist activities.

Bialik in Palestine

Soon after the World War, Bialik settled in Palestine, where he lived until his death in 1934. He wrote few poems during these years, but preferred to devote himself to scholarly work, to publishing Hebrew books, and to communal activities. His home in Tel Aviv was open to everyone. Young and old, writers and workers, prominent leaders, tourists, all came to him for inspiration. School children with their teachers were particularly welcome, and to visit Uncle Bialik, as they called him, was the dream of every child.

The news of his untimely death, at the age of sixty-one, was received with deep sorrow by Jews the world over. Not in many centuries had so great a Hebrew poet arisen to enrich the Hebrew language and literature. He was the acknowledged poet-laureate of the Jewish people. Each year, on Bialik Day, lovers of Hebrew in every Jewish community pay tribute to the memory of the great poet, and express their rejoicing over the revival of Hebrew.

Chapter 14

THE NATIONAL AMERICAN FESTIVALS

TOGETHER with all Americans, the Jews of the United States celebrate the Fourth of July, Thanksgiving Day, Lincoln's Birthday, and the other national holidays. Each festival brings its particular message to all citizens alike. Thanksgiving Day recalls the hardy pioneers who built this country, while the Fourth of July reminds us of the struggle for independence. Washington's Birthday and Lincoln's Birthday offer us an opportunity to draw inspiration from the lives of these great Americans.

As each holiday rolls around, we also like to think of its

particular meaning to us as Jews, and of the Jew's share in the building of America. We like to compare the Fourth of July with Pesach, both being holidays of national birth. On Thanksgiving Day, we remember the influence of the Bible on the Puritans, on the makers of the Constitution, and on American history in general. Each national holiday is an occasion for recalling the ideals of democracy, religious liberty, equality, and justice for which America stands, and which Jews have held dear since ancient times.

We must make a distinction, however, between the national festivals and the Christian religious holidays. Christmas is celebrated as the birthday of Jesus and is therefore a holiday only for Christians. Similarly, Easter, which commemorates the resurrection of Jesus, is an exclusively Christian holiday. Jews who celebrate the Christian religious holidays do so because of ignorance, or lack of self-respect, or thoughtlessness. Many Christians are rightly resentful when they see Jews celebrating Christmas, their most holy day, merely for fun and enjoyment.

LABOR DAY

With Labor Day, on the first Monday in September, begins the year of work. Children go back to school after two months of play and rest. Business men, office employees, and factory workers also have had their vacations and settle down for a year of work. Then, too, Labor Day marks the onset of a new season, summer being practically over.

As a workers' holiday, it is an occasion for mass meetings and conferences by labor organizations to discuss their problems, and to foster cooperation between employers and employees. Parades with uniformed bands march through the main streets of every city and town. Jews take part in these celebrations together with all citizens.

A Jewish Contribution

We recall on Labor Day the large share Jews have had in improving working conditions by organizing labor unions. Jews have been among the pioneers in this field. Two of the most important unions in America, the Amalgamated Clothing Workers of America and the International Women's Garment Workers, have been developed by Jews. To this day they are among the best labor organizations in the country. Jews have been active in the American Federation of Labor and in the Congress for Industrial Organization. Samuel Gompers, a Jew, served as president of the A.F.L. for twenty years. Today, Sidney Hillman is one of the best known labor leaders in the country.

In addition to being members of unions, the Jewish workers have a large and strong organization known as the Arbeiter Ring or Workmen's Circle, and also the National Workers Alliance. These bodies carry on educational and social activities on behalf of their members as well as on behalf of the Jewish community. Similar Jewish labor organizations exist in Poland and in other countries.

This active interest of modern Jews in improving working conditions is not new. As far back as three thousand years ago, the Jews instituted the Sabbath as a day of rest; the commandment to keep the Sabbath is known to be the first labor legislation in the history of the world. At the same time, Jews have treasured work. The biblical saying, "By the sweat of thy brow shalt thou eat bread," has been considered a blessing rather than a curse. "Love labor" taught one of the sages in the Ethics of the Fathers. In

209

modern Palestine, Jews speak of the religion of labor, which means that to work is a privilege and a duty, and that the meanest kind of labor should not be shunned.

Vocational Problems

Thousands of young Jews go out immediately after Labor Day to find jobs. Thousands more in high schools and colleges begin to think seriously what courses to take in order to prepare themselves for earning a livelihood. Before deciding definitely, these boys and girls ask themselves: What opportunities for employment are open to Jews? Do we not have too many Jews in business and in the professions? Why are there so few Jews in the mechanical trades and in agriculture? Is the accusation so often heard — that Jews do not like to work with their hands — true? If true, what can we do about it?

Jewish Labor in Palestine

In Palestine the great majority of Jews are farmers and workers. There Jewish labor is converting a waste land into a fruitful Homeland for the Jewish people. The farm and city workers are organized into a strong union, popularly known as the Histadrut, which protects the interests of its members, furthers cooperation, conducts educational activities, and looks after the health of the workers.

MEMORIAL DAY

Decoration Day was dedicated in 1868, as an occasion for decorating the graves of Civil War soldiers. In time, it has become customary to look after the graves of all soldiers, as well as of relatives and friends, on this day.

THE NATIONAL AMERICAN FESTIVALS

It is now called Memorial Day, when we pay tribute to all who gave their lives for this country. We remember particularly the ideals of liberty and union for which the Civil War soldiers fought, and the ideals of democracy for which Americans were sent to the European battle-fields. In both wars Jews fought side by side with other Americans. The Jewish War Veterans take part in the parades and ceremonies of the day. Jewish schools, clubs, and institutions conduct special programs dealing with the history of American Jews, and with the ideals of freedom, democracy, and justice which are our heritage as Americans and as Jews.

COLUMBUS DAY — DISCOVERY DAY

The discovery of America by Columbus is perhaps the greatest single event in the history of the world during the past thousand years. The anniversary of that discovery, in 1492, is celebrated in the United States, in Latin American countries, and even in some cities of Spain and Italy. The Jews of America join heartily with the millions of people on three continents to express their happiness in this discovery, and to honor the memory of the famous explorer.

Jews Who Helped Columbus

The question whether Columbus was a Jew or not may never be answered definitely. What is known, however, is that Jews played an important part in the discovery. Columbus prepared himself for the voyage by studying the maps and charts of Judah Cresques and the astronomical tables of Abraham Zacuto, both well-known Jewish scholars. Two other Jews, Louis de Santangel and Gabriel Sanchez, helped persuade the king and queen of Spain to

211

furnish the ships for the voyage, and they also gave Columbus their personal funds. These two were Columbus' best friends; his first letter describing the voyage was sent to them. Furthermore, among those who accompanied the explorer were six Jews. One of them, Luis de Torres, acted as interpreter for the fleet, and was the first white man to set foot on American soil.

Haven of Refuge

The date of the famous expedition, 1492, is one of the darkest in the long and eventful history of the Jewish people. In that year the Jews of Spain were given two cruel alternatives — either to be baptized and become Catholics or to be expelled from the country. Most of the 300,000 Jews in Spain chose to leave their native land. It is thought that the ships loaded with Jewish refugees may have sighted Columbus' fleet setting out for America.

Columbus' voyage opened up a new world to mankind, where millions of people from every part of the globe, among them some five million Jews, have found peace, freedom, and security. Today again Jewish as well as Christian refugees from Germany and other countries are seeking a haven of refuge in the land discovered by Columbus.

ARMISTICE DAY OR PEACE DAY

Those who are old enough to remember November 11, 1918 will never forget that day. After four bloody years, armistice was at last declared; the World War was over. Men, women, and children danced in the streets for joy.

And a costly peace it was. During the four years, 8,538,315 young men were killed on the battlefields; 21,219,450 were wounded; how many millions died of starvation and disease will probably never be known. Fabulous sums of money were spent to kill and maim and ruin. The victors forgot to celebrate their victory. They were happy first and foremost because peace had come.

The Jews were among the most joyous people in the world on that day. Not only had peace come to the world and to the Jews as well, but millions of Jews had been freed from tyranny, and Palestine had been promised as the Jewish Homeland. With Armistice Day, they hoped, a new era would dawn for the homeless Jew.

The anniversary of the armistice has come to be known as Peace Day, when we rededicate ourselves to the ideal of peace among nations and races. In the programs, assemblies, and religious services held on that day, Jews seek inspiration from the Bible, the Talmud, the prayerbook, and other great Jewish writings wherein the ideals of peace and brotherhood are so beautifully expressed.

THANKSGIVING DAY

That first harvest festival celebrated by the Pilgrims, in 1621, marked the beginning of practical work to build up the United States of America. They were the earliest pioneers to blaze a trail for the millions who followed them. We observe Thanksgiving Day in honor of the Pilgrims, as well as of all the pioneers who laid the foundations of this great and good country. We recall their bravery, their neighborliness and cooperation in the untamed plains, mountains, and forests, their eagerness to set up schools and houses of worship in every new settlement, and, above all, their ideals of freedom, justice, and respect for the law.

Jewish Holidays and Festivals

In laying the foundations of a new nation, the Pilgrim Fathers were greatly influenced by Jewish teachings in the Bible. We need but examine their first names — Gamaliel, Ezekiel, Samuel, and the like — to realize how deep this influence was. Many of the laws made by them, as well as the form of government planned, were inspired by the Torah, for they read and studied the Old Testament no less than the New Testament. They sang many of the Psalms on the first Thanksgiving. Jews may truly say, therefore, that they were represented, in spirit if not in body, on that memorable day.

The uppermost thought in the minds of Jews on this holiday is one of thanksgiving for the new "promised land," where over a fourth of the Jewish people has found peace and freedom. What would have happened to the millions of Jews had they been compelled to remain in Europe? And who would have saved the millions of European Jews during and after the World War if there had not been a large and strong American Jewry? Who today could be relied upon to aid Jewish victims of the new war and of Nazi persecutions? No one is more thankful on Thanksgiving Day than the refugees who have recently come to America.

The custom itself — the idea of a harvest festival — is not new to the Jewish people. Jews have always observed two harvest festivals — Shavuot and Succot. There is good reason to believe that the Puritans modeled Thanksgiving Day after the Jewish festival of Succot. Today, when Jews are tilling the soil once again in Palestine, it is natural that on Thanksgiving Day we should compare the American pioneers with the HALUTZIM who are rebuilding the Jewish Homeland.

LINCOLN'S BIRTHDAY

Abraham Lincoln is the great national hero of every American. All citizens, no matter what their race or religion, pay tribute to the great emancipator on the anniversary of his birthday. The story of his life — how he worked hard to acquire an education, how gradually he was recognized for the great man he was, and how under his leadership liberty and the union were saved — is an inspiration to young and old.

We like to think that he was inspired by the teachings of the Old Testament. For surely the family would not have named him Abraham if the Bible had not been a sacred book to them. Lincoln himself read and studied the Holy Scriptures many times, and he must have known well the story of the enslavement of the Hebrews in Egypt and how they freed themselves under the leadership of Moses.

Like Washington, Lincoln believed that the full rights of citizenship were meant for everybody. It happened during the Civil War that General Grant ordered all traders, including "the Jews as a class," to leave the district under his command. Jewish representatives protested to Lincoln against this order, and against singling out the Jews. Lincoln at once revoked the order. He was equally ready to pardon a Jewish soldier for deserting the army in order to be at the side of his dying mother. Among Lincoln's supporters and friends were several Jews of prominence.

When honoring the memory of Lincoln, we also recall the part Jews played in the Civil War. There were altogether about 200,000 Jews then in America. The number of Jewish soldiers was close to 7,500, of whom over 6,000 fought in the Northern army. One Jew in particular distinguished himself — Judah P. Benjamin — who served as secretary of three departments in the Confederate cabinet. The great majority of Jews were on the side of Union and liberty, for these ideals have been part of Judaism since ancient times.

WASHINGTON'S BIRTHDAY

When George Washington accepted command of the Revolutionary Army, there were only about 3,000 Jews in the thirteen colonies. They could not be a strong force in the struggle for independence. Quite a number served in the army, among them several who distinguished themselves for heroism. Men of wealth gave generously to help finance the Revolution. One of them, Haym Solomon, played a very important role in obtaining money for Washington, and also gave generously of his own.

The Jews of the time, in their admiration of Washington, probably compared him with Jewish heroes, perhaps with Joshua, Nehemiah, and Judas Maccabeus. The comparison with Judas is especially interesting. Both headed small armies against a much stronger power, in the name of freedom and independence. Both were great generals who led their people to victory.

The memory of Washington is honored each year not only because the thirteen colonies were victorious, but also because of his personality and ideals which Americans have admired ever since. To this day, presidents and statesmen ask themselves when difficult questions arise: What would George Washington have done in such a case? He has been an example and inspiration to every generation.

THE NATIONAL AMERICAN FESTIVALS

Washington's Message

Immediately after Washington's election as President, the six Jewish congregations then in existence sent him letters of congratulations and good wishes. His replies show how much he was influenced by the Bible, and they express his ideals of tolerance, equality, and freedom for all inhabitants of the United States. This is part of the letter he wrote to the Jews of Newport: "May the children of the stock of Abraham who dwell in this land continue to merit and enjoy the good will of the other inhabitants, while everyone shall sit under his own vine and fig tree, and there shall be none to make him afraid." We should remember that these words were written a century and a half ago, when the ideals of tolerance, equality, and liberty were only beginning to emerge.

FOURTH OF JULY

To the Jews, Independence Day has a special meaning. On the day when the Declaration of Independence was adopted, the Jews of the world were still living in ghettos. Nowhere were they considered full citizens, entitled to all the rights and privileges enjoyed by other inhabitants. The United States was the first country to make no distinction between Jew and non-Jew. The Declaration of Independence was meant for all alike. Several years later, France and Holland granted similar rights to their Jews. In some countries, however, as in Russia, Jews had to wait for full citizenship until the World War. Sad to say, Germany, Italy, Hungary, and other countries have in recent years taken away the rights of citizenship from the Jewish people.

Jews like to compare the Fourth of July to Passover. On

both festivals we celebrate the birth of a nation. On Pesach we commemorate the Exodus from Egypt, when a new nation was created, one that has existed for over three thousand years and has made great contributions to the world. Each Independence Day we celebrate the birth of a great nation, one that has led the world in ideals of democracy, religious freedom, equality, and justice. On the Fourth of July we rededicate ourselves to the ideals of democracy, because as Americans and as Jews we believe democracy to be the best way of life. We know, too, that only in a democratic country can Jews enjoy freedom and peace.

Bibliography

THE following list is not intended to be exhaustive but rather to indicate the more useful books containing information about the holidays, as well as collections of literary material and festival songs.

Abrahams, Israel, *Festival Studies*
Abrahams, Israel, *Jewish Life in the Middle Ages*
Agnon, S., *Yamim Noraim* (Hebrew)
Dembitz. Lewis, N., *Services in Synagogue and Home*
Doniach, N. S., *Purim*
Edidin, Ben M., *Rebuilding Palestine*, Ch. xvi
Eisenstein, Ira, *What Religion Means to Us*
Friedlander, Gerald, *Laws and Customs of Israel*
Friedlander, M., *Jewish Religion*
Greenstone, Julius, H., *The Jewish Religion*
Hertz, J. H., *The Pentateuch and Haftorahs*. See Index for Holidays
Idelsohn, A. Z., *The Ceremonies of Judaism*
Joseph, Morris, *Judaism as Creed and Life*
Kaplan, Mordecai M., *The Meaning of God in Modern Jewish Religion*
Lehrman, S. W., *Jewish Festivals*
Melamed, Deborah, *The Three Pillars*
Mendes, H. P., *Jewish Religion*
Moore, George Foot, *Judaism*, Vols. i, ii
Pardo, Joseph, *Abridged Shulhan Arukh*
Rappoport, Angelo S., *The Folklore of the Jews*
Rosenau, Wm., *Jewish Ceremonial Institutions*
Schauss, *The Jewish Festivals*
Schechter, A. I., *Symbols and Ceremonies*
Soltes, Mordecai, *The Jewish Holidays*

Encyclopedia of Jewish Knowledge
The Jewish Encyclopedia

BIBLIOGRAPHY

STORIES, LEGENDS, PLAYS, ETC.:

Baruch, J. L., *Sefer Hashabbat*, (Hebrew); Edidin, Ben M., *Hanukah, Pesach, Shavuot*, Jewish Child Home Library; Harari, Hayim, *Sefer Hanukah*, (Hebrew); Goldin, Hyman, E., *Holiday Tales*; Levinger E. E., *Jewish Festivals in Religious Schools*; Sachs, A. S., *Worlds That Passed*; Salaman, Nina, *Apples and Honey*; Shalom Aleichem, *Jewish Children*; Solis-Cohen, Emily, *Hanukah*; *Holiday Programs*, issued by Bureaus of Jewish Education, Jewish Welfare Board, Young Judaea, and other educational agencies.

HOLIDAY POEMS AND SONGS:

Friedlander, Joseph, *Standard Book of Jewish Verse*; Kohut, George A., *A Hebrew Anthology*; Raskin, Philip, *Anthology of Modern Poetry*; Young Judaea, *Poems for Young Judaeans*.

Coopersmith, Harry, *Jewish Community Songster, Songs of My People*; Goldfarb, Israel and Samuel, *The Jewish Songster*, Vols. I, II; Nathanson, Moshe, *Shireynu* and *Manginoth Shireynu*.

BOOKS FOR YOUNG CHILDREN:

Braverman, Libbie L., *Children of the Emek*; Eisenstein, Judith K., *Gateway to Jewish Song*; Gamoran, Mamie, *Hillel's Happy Holidays*; King, Marian, *A Lad of Palestine*; Levinger, E. E., *Jewish Holiday Stories*; Levinger, E. E., *With the Jewish Child at Home and Synagogue*; Mazer, Sonia, *Yossele's Holiday*; Sampter, Jessie, *Around the Year in Rhymes*; Trager, Hannah, *Festival Stories*; Willerstein, S. R., *What Danny Did*.

Index and Glossary

KEY TO PRONUNCIATION

ALL Hebrew terms in this index as well as throughout the book are spelled in accordance with the Sephardic pronunciation commonly used in Palestine. Pronounce: "a," as in father; "o," as in more; "e," as in met; "u," as in put; "i," as in hit.

Adar, month of, 118f.
Adloyada, Purim festivities in Tel Aviv, 126ff.
Afikoman, 145, 147
Agricultural festivals. See Pesach, Shavuot, Succot, Hamishah Asar.
Ahasuerus, 117ff.
Akedah, offering of Isaac, 49, 51, 53
Akiba, Rabbi Joseph Ben, 63, 155ff. 162, 169, 181
Al Hanisim prayer, 95
Amnon, Rabbi of Mayence, 50f.
Antiochus, 88f.
Arabs, 182, 198
Armistice Day, 42, 212f.
Asarah Betevet, Tenth of Tevet, fast, 179, 186f.
Aseret Yemey Teshuvah, Ten Days of Penitence, 55f.
Ashkenazim, Western Jews, 143
Avodah, Sacred Service on Yom Kippur, 65

Babylonian customs, comparison with 18, 38
Balfour Declaration Day, 194ff.
Balfour Declaration, the, 195f.
Bar Cochba, 63, 155ff., 181
Bar Mitzvah, 14, 20, 25, 28f., 166, 182
Bar Yohai, Simeon, 155f., 158, 161f.

Basle Program of Zionism, 193
Bedikat Hametz, clearing out the Hametz, 141
Besamim, spices, refers to Havdalah spice box, 26
Bialik Day, 202ff.
Bialik, Hayyim Nahman, 31, 202ff.
Bible, observance in Bible times, 18f., 35f., 54, 70f., 133ff., 166f.
Bible, reading from. See Torah and Haftorah.
Bikkurim, First Fruits, 38, 167ff.
Birkat Hamazon, Grace after meals, 24
Biur Hametz, burning of the Hametz, 141
Blessing children, custom of, 59f.
Blood accusation, 138
Bonfires, on Lag Beomer, 37

Calendar, Jewish, 36f. 39, 53f., 107f., 166
Carnivals on Purim, See Adloyada
Cemetery, visiting of, 48, 56, 182, 185
Christian holidays, 18, 54f., 208
Columbus Day, 211ff.
Commencement Day, 109
Community celebrations, 14, 31f., 78f., 99, 126ff., 129, 149, 160, 172, 194

221

INDEX

Contributions, for the poor, to Jewish funds, 22, 42, 57, 58, 98, 114, 122, 124, 130, 140, 184

Dreidel, Hanukah top, 97
Dreyfus trial, 191

Elijah, the prophet, 27, 144, 147f.
Eretz Yisrael. See Palestine.
Erev Shabbat, day before the Sabbath, 21
Esther, 177ff.
Esther, Book of. See Megillah.
Ethics of the Fathers, book of 25, 209
Etrog, citron, 72, 75f., 78, 79, 83
Exodus, from Egypt, 18, 54, 71, 131ff., 170, 172, 180
Exodus, Book of, 132ff.

Falashas, Jews of Ethiopia, 28f.
Fasting and Fast Days, 58f., 179ff.
Feast of Weeks. See Shavuot.
First fruits. See Bikkurim.
Fish, symbolism of, 49, 53
Flowers, on Sabbath and holidays, 30, 166, 172ff.
Forgiveness, custom of begging forgiveness, 58
Four Questions, of the Haggadah, 137, 145
"Four Species," Lulav, Etrog, myrtle and willow used on Succot, 72, 75ff.
Fourth of July, 207, 217f.
Fruits of Palestine, 109f.

Games, on holidays, 21, 25, 97, 129, 142, 149, 160
Gedaliah, Fast of, 56, 179, 181
Geshem, prayer for rain, 80
Ghetto, celebrations in. See Middle Ages.
Gifts, on holidays, 97, 98, 110, 122, 124f. 128f.

Great Britain, aid Palestine, 195f.
Greeks, 88f.
Greetings, on High Holy Days, 48, 62
Grager, Purim rattle, 123, 129

Had Gadya, An Only Kid, song, 148
Haftorahs, readings from the Prophets on Sabbaths and Holidays, 25, 53, 56, 64, 78, 150, 182, 186
Haggadah, story. Book used at the Seder, 13, 139, 142, 144f.
Haifa, celebrations in, 31, 175f.
Hakafot, Procession with the Scrolls on Simhat Torah, 82f.
Hallot, Sabbath and holiday loaves, 19, 22, 24, 48, 57, 77
Halutzim, pioneers, 31, 75f., 102, 151, 197f.
Haman, 117ff., 159
Hamantaschen, Purim cakes, 125, 128f.
Hametz, leavened bread, 140f.
Hamishah Asar Bishevat, Fifteenth of Shevat. New Year of the Trees in Palestine, 10, 54, 105ff.
Hannah, 91, 96
Hanukah, Dedication, Festival of Lights, 10, 87ff.
Hanukah Gelt, Hanukah money. 97
Hanukiyah, Hanukah lamp, 95ff.
Haroset, mixture of nuts, apple and wine used at Seder, 143
Harvest Festivals. See Shavuot, Succot.
Hasidim, pious ones, 89f., 102
Hasmoneans, 91ff., 101
Hatarat Nedarim, ceremony of release from vows, 47
Havdalah, separation, ceremony of farewell to the Sabbath, 26f., 31f., 67
Hazan, cantor, 23, 25, 40, 82

INDEX

Hebrew Language, 13, 89f., 196, 200, 202ff.
Hebrew University, the, 199f.
Hebrew University Day, 199ff.
Hellenists, Jews who adopted Greek customs, 89f., 102
Herzl Day, 190ff.
Herzl, Dr. Theodor, 190ff., 194f.
High Holy Days, 45ff. See also Rosh Hashanah, Yom Kippur.
High Priest, 36, 65, 90f.
Hol Hamoed, the days between the first and last days of Pesach and of Succot, 78f., 149
Home, observance in the, 22f., 24ff., 40, 48f., 57ff., 68, 77, 95ff., 110, 123ff., 140ff., 160
Honey, custom of dipping bread or fruit in, 55, 77, 165
Horah, Palestinian folk dance, 10
Hoshana Rabba, Great Help, seventh day of Succot, 73, 77
Hovevey Zion, Lovers of Zion, 192
Humash, Five Books of Moses, 81

Inquisition, in Spain, 14, 60, 138
Iyar, month of, 158, 159

Jerusalem. See Temple, observance in.
Jewish Book Day, 162
Jewish National Fund. See Keren Kayemet.
"Jewish State", the, Book written by Dr. Herzl, 191f.
Judith, story of, 96.

Kaparot, sacrificial ceremony on day before Yom Kippur, 57f.
Karaite Jews, 28
Keren Kayemet, Jewish National Fund, 42, 84, 99, 114, 122, 130, 163, 175, 193, 199
Kiddush, prayer, on Sabbath and major holidays, 23, 77, 144

Kiddush Halevanah, Sanctification of the Moon ceremony, 41, 68
Kinnot, dirges or lamentations, 185
Kittel, white robe worn on Yom Kippur, also at the Seder, 60
Kohanim or priests. See Temple.
Kohelet, or Book of Ecclesiastes, 78
Kol Nidre, prayer on Yom Kippur, 59f.
Kosher, ritually fit to eat, 30

Labor Day, 208ff.
Lag Beomer, thirty-three days in Omer, 10, 155ff., 189. See also Omer.
Lamentations, Book of, read on Tishah Beav, 184
Lechah Dodi, Sabbath prayer, 23
Lincoln's Birthday, 207, 215f.
Levites. See Temple
Lulav, palm leaf used on Succot, 72, 75f., 78, 79, 80, 83

Maccabees, 11, 19, 88f., 92f., 102, 216
Maccabees, Books of, 93
Mahzor, prayerbook for holidays, 47, 49f., 56, 62f.
Maimonides, Moses, 52, 58, 75
Maot Hittim, coins for wheat, fund for helping the poor celebrate Pesach, 140
Maoz Tzur, Rock of Ages, Hanukah hymn, 95f.
Maror, bitter herbs used on Pesach, 143
Marranos, converted Jews who kept Judaism in secret, 29
Masquerades on Purim, 126ff.
Mattathias, 91, 101
Matzot, unleavened cakes, 134ff.
Megillah, scroll, reading of, 123ff, 129
Megillat Antiochus, Scroll of Antiochus, 94

INDEX

Melaveh Malkah, Farewell to Queen Sabbath ceremony, 27, 34
Memorial Day, 179f., 210f.
Memorial Services, 64f., 80, 179
Menorah, 12, 22f., 48, 51, 57, 77, 88. See also Hanukiyah
Meron, festival of, on Lag Beomer, 161f.
Messiah, Messianic Times, 11, 27, 72, 119, 172, 185f., 187f.
Mezuzah, sacred object on door posts, 13
Middle Ages, observance during, 20f., 94ff., 108, 137f., 184
Mitzvah, commandment, good deed, 20, 22, 31, 83, 113
Modin, town where Maccabees lived, 91, 101
Molad, birth of new moon, 40
Mordecai, 118ff.
Mordecai's letter, to the Jews, 119
Moses, 132f.
Mourning, mourners, 20, 30, 182ff.
Myrtle, or Hadas, attached to Lulav, 20, 72, 75f.

Neilah, closing service on Yom Kippur, 66f.
Neshamah Yeterah, over-soul, 32
New Moon, meaning of, 38f.
New Year. See Rosh Hashanah.
Nisan, month of, 53, 136, 139

Omer, sheaf or measure of grain, 133, 150, 151f., 157f., 166
Oneg Shabbat, Sabbath Joy, new Sabbath custom, 31f.
Oriental Jews, observance among, 28f., 66, 73, 83, 109f., 122f., 148f., 185.

Palestine, observance of holidays in, 15, 30f., 35f., 41f., 83f., 99ff., 111ff., 150f., 161f., 174ff.

Paschal lamb, 133f., 143
Pentateuch, Five Books of Moses, 29, 83
Peri Etz Hadar, Fruit of the Citrus Tree, name of book read on Hamishah Asar, 109
Persia, Jews of, customs among, 117ff., 160f.
Pesach Passover, 9, 10, 13, 38, 54, 70, 131ff., 158, 166, 183
Pharaoh, 132, 146
Pilgrimages, Pilgrims, 56, 70f., 72, 136f., 167f.
Piyutim, hymns of praise, 49, 63
Planting Trees in Palestine on Hamishah Asar, 106f., 110ff.
Plays on holidays. See Community celebrations.
Prayerbook, 12, 25. See also Mahzor.
Priests or Kohanim. See Temple.
Purim, 10, 11, 81, 117ff.
Purim of Cairo, 121
Purim of Vincenz, 121
Purim Spielers, or minstrels, 125f.

Rachel, Tomb of, 56
Rome, Romans, and Palestine, 37, 39, 54, 156f., 169, 181
Rosh Hashanah, New Year, 10, 11, 38, 45ff.
Rosh Hashanah Leilanot, New Year of the Trees. See Hamishah Asar Bishevat.
Rosh Hodesh, New Moon or first of the month, 35ff.
Ruth, Book of, 173

Sabbath, the, 9, 10, 11, 17ff., 34, 39, 46, 89. 209f.
Sabbath greetings, 23, 24
Sabbaths, special, 27, 39f.
Sacrifices, in ancient times, 19, 36, 39, 58, 65, 70, 88, 133f., 137, 167f.
Samaritans, 133

INDEX

Sanhedrin, name of supreme court and legislative body in ancient Palestine, 37f.

Scholars' Day, Lag Beomer, 158, 162

Schools, observance of holidays by Jewish, 25, 42, 43, 78f., 88, 100f., 108f., 126, 149, 160, 172f., 174, 204f.

Seder, the, 13, 133, 138, 142ff.

Selihot, prayers of repentance, 46f., 57

Sephardim, Jews of Spanish origin, 143. See also Oriental Jews.

Sephirah, counting days between Pesach and Shavuot, 159f., 166

Seudah, or feast held on Purim, 124f., 129

Seudah Shelishit, Third meal on Sabbath afternoon, 24, 26, 31

Shabbat Hagadol, Great Sabbath, preceding Pesach, 27, 139

Shabbat Hazon, Sabbath before Tishah Beav, 27, 182f.

Shabbat Mevarchim, Sabbath when new month is announced, 27

Shabbat Nahamu, Sabbath of Comforting, 27, 186

Shabbat Shirah, Sabbath of Song, 27

Shabbat Shuvah, Sabbath of Repentance, 27, 50f.

Shalachmanot, sending gifts on Purim, 124f., 128f.

Shalom Aleichem, Peace Unto You, Sabbath hymn, 24, 41

Shanah Tovah greeting cards, 47

Shavuot, Feast of Weeks, 10, 11, 38, 54, 70, 81, 158, 165ff., 214

Shemini Atzeret, Eighth Day of Solemn Assembly, 80f.

Shevat, month of, 105f.

Shivah Asar Betamuz, fast on seventeenth of Tamuz, 186

Shofar, 36, 37, 39, 46, 51ff., 67

Shushan Purim, 119

Sidrah, portion of the week, 24, 81

Simhat Bet Hashoevah, Festival of the Water-pouring, 78

Simhat Torah, 81ff., 117, 171

Solemn Season, Yamim Noraim, 46ff.

Sopherim, Scribes, 19

Spain, Jews in, 21, 138, 181

Spring festivals, 105ff., 134

Succah, 68, 71ff., 80f.

Succot, booths or Tabernacles, 10, 11, 38, 54, 69ff., 88, 167, 214

Survival of Jews, 14

Synagogue, observance in, 19, 23f., 25, 29, 40, 46f., 49ff., 60ff., 77f., 79ff., 94f., 109f., 122ff., 150, 172, 184f.

Taanit Esther, Fast of Esther, 179, 187

Tal, dew, prayer for, 150

Talmud, observance in Talmudic times, 19f., 37f., 65f., 72f., 106f., 167ff.

Talmud, quotations from, 19f., 27, 42, 72, 75, 93, 106f., 119, 132, 167f., 169f.

Targum Sheni, book of Purim folklore, 120

Tashlich, Rosh Hashanah ceremony, 52

Tel Aviv, celebrations in, 31, 100f., 111ff., 126ff., 162

Tel Hai, colony in Palestine, 197f.

Temple, observance in ancient, 11, 22f., 36f., 39, 65f., 71ff., 78, 87ff., 135ff., 156, 167f.

Ten Commandments, 11, 17, 52, 81, 170ff.

Thanksgiving Day, 207, 213f.

"Three Weeks," before Tishah Beav, 182f., 186

Tishah Beav, 27, 179ff.

Tithe, tax in ancient Palestine, 107f.

Torah, importance of, 69, 81, 155ff. 165ff., 214

225

INDEX

Torah reading of, 20, 27, 40, 49, 53, 63, 77, 81f., 150, 171f.
Tree certificate, of Jewish National Fund, 114
Trees, of Palestine, 106f.
Trendel, Hanukah top, 97
Trumpeldor Day, 197ff.
Trumpeldor, Joseph, 197ff.
Two Days of Holiday, 37f.
Tzedakah, or charity customs. See Contributions.

Unetaneh Tokef, prayer, 50f., 63
Ushpizin, song to Succot guests, 77

Venice, Hanukah in old, 94f.
Vineyard Festival, on Yom Kippur, 66

Wailing Wall, 31, 48, 185
Washington's Birthday, 207, 216f.
Weizmann, Dr. Chaim, 42, 199f. 201
Willows, or Hoshanot, used on Succot, 72, 75f., 79
World War, 194f.

Yemenite Jews, 28f., 98, 173. See also Oriental Jews.
Yom Kippur, Day of Atonement, 9, 10, 11, 20, 29, 45, 57ff., 79, 179, 183
Yom Tov, holiday or festival, 77

Zemirot, Sabbath chants, 25, 31f.
Zionism, and Zionist organization, 190ff.